Fodor's

25 Best

SINGAPORE

How to Use This Book

KEY TO SYMBOLS

- Map reference to the accompanying fold-out map
- Address
- Telephone number
- Opening/closing times
- Restaurant or café
- Nearest rail station
- Nearest MRT station
- Nearest bus route
- Nearest riverboat or ferry stop
- Facilities for visitors with disabilities
- Other practical information
- ▷ Further information
- Tourist information
- Admission charges: Expensive (over S$16), Moderate (S$8–S$15), and Inexpensive (S$7 or less)

This guide is divided into four sections

• Essential Singapore: An introduction to the city and tips on making the most of your stay.

• Singapore by Area: We've broken the city into four areas, and recommended the best sights, shops, entertainment venues, nightlife and restaurants in each one. Suggested walks help you to explore on foot.

• Where to Stay: The best hotels, whether you're looking for luxury, budget or something in between.

• Need to Know: The info you need to make your trip run smoothly, including getting about by public transport, weather tips, emergency phone numbers and useful websites.

Navigation In the Singapore by Area chapter, we've given each area its own tint, which is also used on the locator maps throughout the book and the map on the inside front cover.

Maps The fold-out map accompanying this book is a comprehensive street plan of central Singapore. The grid on this map is the same as the grid on The City area locator map and has upper case grid references. Sights and listings within the East Island and West Island areas have lower case grid references.

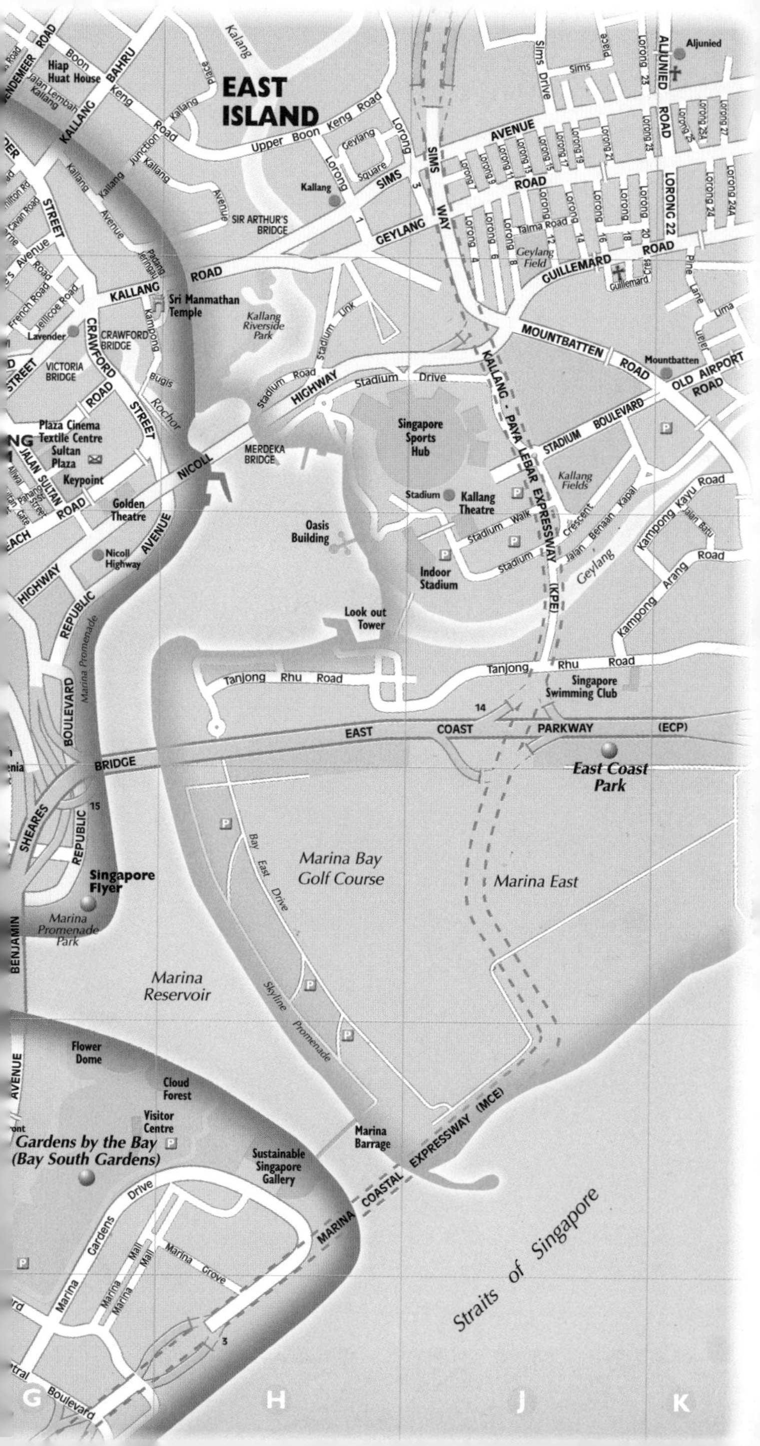
EAST ISLAND
Hiap Huat House
Kallang
Kallang Riverside Park
Sri Manmathan Temple
Lavender
CRAWFORD BRIDGE
VICTORIA BRIDGE
SIR ARTHUR'S BRIDGE
MERDEKA BRIDGE
Plaza Cinema
Textile Centre
Sultan Plaza
Keypoint
Golden Theatre
Nicoll Highway
Singapore Sports Hub
Stadium
Kallang Theatre
Oasis Building
Indoor Stadium
Look out Tower
Kallang Fields
Geylang Field
Singapore Swimming Club
East Coast Park
Mountbatten
Aljunied
Marina Bay Golf Course
Marina East
Singapore Flyer
Marina Promenade Park
Marina Reservoir
Flower Dome
Cloud Forest
Visitor Centre
Gardens by the Bay (Bay South Gardens)
Sustainable Singapore Gallery
Marina Barrage
Straits of Singapore
NICOLL HIGHWAY
KALLANG ROAD
GEYLANG ROAD
SIMS AVENUE
SIMS WAY
GUILLEMARD ROAD
MOUNTBATTEN ROAD
OLD AIRPORT ROAD
STADIUM BOULEVARD
KALLANG - PAYA LEBAR EXPRESSWAY (KPE)
EAST COAST PARKWAY (ECP)
MARINA COASTAL EXPRESSWAY (MCE)
Tanjong Rhu Road
Bay East Drive
Skyline Promenade
Marina Gardens Drive
BENJAMIN SHEARES BRIDGE
REPUBLIC BOULEVARD
REPUBLIC AVENUE
ALJUNIED ROAD
LORONG 22
G
H
J
K

Contents

Introducing Singapore

The tiny island nation of Singapore is a dramatic fusion of the Victorian age and the 21st century. It's morphed from destitute and war-ravaged ex-colony into an affluent, educated and savvy nation—a change that's been carried out with verve and style.

Tree-lined avenues, landscaped urban areas, small parks and roadside tropical greenery are common features of this attractive, tidy city. Building on an illustrious trading history, Singapore is the world's busiest shipping port, and rivalled only by Tokyo as Asia's premier financial hub. Despite the island's impressive development, seen in the cityscape of tower blocks, freeways and glitzy malls, Singapore retains a fairly laid-back feel and pockets of the old world remain in superbly restored (or occasionally rebuilt) areas.

The diversity of race—Chinese, Malay, Indians, plus workers from other parts of Asia and the West—and their many religions, festivals and cultural practices is where Singapore sets itself apart. Ancient imported traditions remain important but a strong Singaporean identity has been forged in the country's rapid development, and relations between the races are better than many other cosmopolitan cities.

Lying just over 60 miles (100km) north of the equator, the island has a tropical climate, with a humidity, often above 90 per cent, that can sap the energy of most. Fortunately, air-conditioning rules in shops, hotels and public transportation facilities.

So board a bus, hop on the MRT or hail a cab and explore the delights of this vibrant island state. The neighborhoods each have a distinct character based on their ethnic or colonial origins. Visit the temples of Chinatown, the markets in Little India and the sheesh cafés in Kampong Glam, and Singapore will reveal itself as much more than the shopping frenzy of Orchard Road.

Facts + Figures

- Population in 1819: 500; population in 2012: 5.3 million
- Religions: Taoist/Buddhist 44%; Muslim 15%; Christian 18%; Hindu 5%; other/none 18%

SINGLISH

You're bound to come across Singlish, the local colloquial English, if you talk to many Singaporeans. You'll know someone is speaking Singlish if they throw the word *lah* in at every opportunity to show emphasis. Other examples include: *fli-end* (friend), *tok kong* (very good) and *lerf* (love).

SURROUNDING ISLANDS

While the best-known island is the recreational Sentosa (▷ 62–63), once a British fort, the country is surrounded by more than 50 small islands. They're mostly occupied by the military, oil refineries or nature reserves, but St. John's Island (▷ 98) in the south is a picnic destination and Kusu Island has a turtle sanctuary.

A FINE CITY

You may have heard that Singapore is a fine city (you can even buy the T-shirt). The government's perfectly reasonable campaign to keep the city clean, and its citizens socially responsible, has led to fines of up to S$1,000 for such acts as littering, jaywalking or even failure to flush a public toilet.

A Short Stay in Singapore

DAY 1

Morning Have an early breakfast and head for the **Botanic Gardens** (▷ 56–57) for a walk among the extensive plant collection. Only a few minutes' bus ride from bustling Orchard Road, this tropical botanical treasure-trove is at its best in the cool of the morning.

Mid-morning Take a bus or taxi back into the city and stroll along **Orchard Road** (▷ 36–37). The morning is less crowded than the afternoon and you can always come back when you've found your way around this mega collection of stores.

Lunch Make your way to **Chinatown** (▷ 27) for lunch, after a shower and freshen-up in your hotel. There are many authentic hawker centers here for a quintessential Singapore lunch with the locals.

Afternoon Explore Chinatown's back streets where there are many antique and gift shops—be sure to visit the **Chinatown Heritage Centre** (▷ 26). Wander down South Bridge Road to view three restored shop-houses and the gigantic **Buddha Tooth Relic Temple** (▷ 26).

Mid-afternoon Take a bus or taxi to the **Asian Civilisations Museum** (▷ 24–25) and learn about Asian cultures from the excellent displays in this perfectly restored old colonial-period building.

Dinner Cross Cavenagh Bridge and enjoy a waterside meal at one of the seafood restaurants along Boat Quay.

Evening Head back across the river to the **Esplanade Theatres** (▷ 42) for a performance. Wander over to Marina Bay Sands (▷ 34) and admire the skyline from Ku Dé Ta bar (▷ 48).

DAY 2

Morning Visit **Raffles Hotel** (▷ 38) at the start of the day, a quieter time to wander around one of the world's most famous hotels, when you can enjoy a coffee instead of an expensive Singapore Sling. Check out some of the public spaces, including the famed Long Bar. Then head to the nearby **Singapore Art Museum** (▷ 39), housed in a beautifully restored 19th-century school building, which has a fine collection of Southeast Asian art.

Mid-morning Take a bus or the MRT to Serangoon Road to browse the shops that line the narrow footpaths of **Little India** (▷ 32–33).

Lunch Serangoon Road has plenty of Indian dining options, but a really economical and tasty lunch can be had at **Komala Vilas** (▷ 51).

Afternoon Take the MRT to Bayfront and explore **Gardens by the Bay** (▷ 28–29), filled with a futuristic grove of "Supertrees".

Mid-afternoon Catch the MRT from Bayfront to **Clarke Quay** (▷ 27). Explore the shops around Clarke Quay and perhaps take a boat ride on the Singapore River.

Dinner The riverside setting of **Clarke Quay** (▷ 27), illuminated by the city lights, makes a perfect evening meal destination. Expatriates congregate here after a hard day at the office for drinks and to dine. There are any number of fine dining options along the river.

Evening There are some good nightspots nearby, but try **Zouk** (▷ 49) for top DJs from around the world. **The Pump Room** (▷ 49) is a slightly more chilled out, but no less hip, alternative.

Top 25

TOP 25

►►►

Asian Civilisations Museum ▷ 24–25 Asian history and culture in two stunning buildings.

Botanic Gardens ▷ 56–57 Superbly landscaped gardens full of tropical and subtropical flora.

The Changi Museum ▷ 82 A moving record of conditions endured by prisoners held during WWII.

Singapore Zoo ▷ 70–71 Often hailed as one of the loveliest zoos in the world.

Singapore Science Centre ▷ 68–69 The Science Centre introduces children to science and technology in an entertaining hands-on style.

Singapore Nature Reserves ▷ 66–67 Escape the city to tropical open spaces.

Singapore Flyer ▷ 40 There are spectacular views across Singapore from the world's largest observation wheel.

Singapore Discovery Centre ▷ 64 A fascinating, world-class "edutainment" attraction.

Singapore Art Museum ▷ 39 Local and Asian art is beautifully displayed at this state-of-the-art gallery.

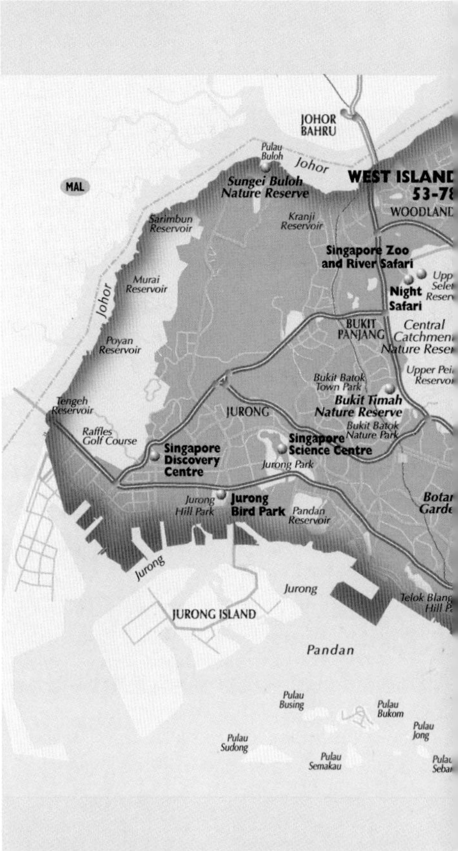

Sentosa ▷ 62–63 An island playground reached via a fabulous cable-car ride.

Raffles Hotel ▷ 38 One of the world's greatest palace-hotels, the cool epitome of colonial style.

Pulau Ubin ▷ 96–97 An offshore island idyll offering a chance to get away from it all.

▲▲▲

These pages are a quick guide to the Top 25, which are described in more detail later. Here they are listed alphabetically, and the tinted background shows which area they are in.

Chinatown ▷ 26
Conveys something of the flavor of old Singapore with its shophouses and alleys.

Clarke Quay ▷ 27
The renovated quayside is most popular as a night-time venue.

East Coast Park ▷ 84–85
Singaporeans head to this beachside area for land and sea sports or to just chill.

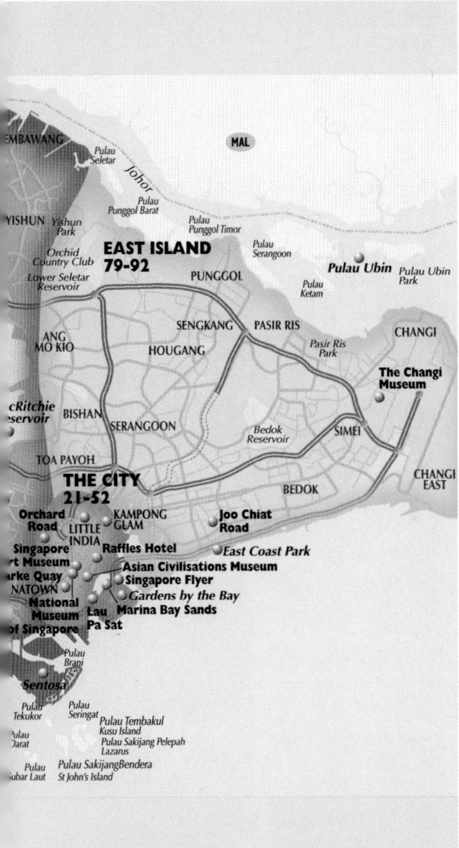

Gardens by the Bay ▷ 28–29 Integrated resort that is home to the world's largest indoor waterfall.

Joo Chiat Road ▷ 83
The traditional Singapore way of life can still be seen in this nostalgic area.

Jurong Bird Park ▷ 58–59 Home to more than 9,000 birds from all over the world.

Kampong Glam ▷ 30
Historic district named after the glam tree.

Lau Pa Sat ▷ 31
Food stalls line a Victorian cast-iron building

Little India ▷ 32–33 The exotic sights, sounds and smells of southern India.

Marina Bay Sands ▷ 34
An iconic part of the city-scape filled with celebrity chef restaurants.

Orchard Road ▷ 36–37
A tree-lined boulevard offering some of Singapore's best shopping.

Night Safari ▷ 60–61
Take the tram ride around this park and see creatures in their night-time habitats.

National Museum of Singapore ▷ 35
Singapore's history comes to life here.

Shopping

Shopping in Singapore is a very serious activity. Without a doubt, the city is Southeast Asia's shopping capital and shops seem to outnumber its inhabitants.

Singapore's Orchard Road (▷ 36–37) provides a comprehensive shopping experience equal to other world capitals, and is particularly recommended for brand-name fashion goods, electronics and cameras. But the benefit of Singapore shopping to those interested in ethnic arts and crafts or Asian antiques is that the nation state's racial mix of Chinese, Malay and Indian means that all types of goods from these cultures can be found in the specialist shops, especially those in the different ethnic quarters of the city. From the Chinese area you will find porcelain, masks, silk and traditional paintings; from the Malay there's basketware, Ikat cloth, batiks, puppets, sarongs and leatherware; and from the Indian quarter paintings, jewelry, sculptures and pottery.

Not surprisingly, given Singapore's hot and humid weather, every large building has air-conditioning. Major Orchard Road department stores include Tangs, Robinsons and Takashimaya. Be sure to check out Far East Plaza in Scotts Road for younger fashions. For small, inexpensive souvenirs, take the MRT to Bugis. For cameras and electronic equipment try Lucky Plaza and Sim Lim Square, armed with your STB good retailers guide (▷ 11) and the Funan Digitalife Mall on North Bridge Road. The huge Marina Square, including

DUTY-FREE LAWS

Singapore's Tourist Refund Scheme means you can claim back 7 per cent Goods and Services Tax on large purchases when you depart from Chaingi Airport. Whenever you spend more than S$100 with a single retailer in a single day, ask for a copy of the GST tax refund form and present it to airport customs officials to claim your refund.

Singapore's shopping is some of the best in the world—particularly along the famous Orchard Road

Millenia Walk, five minutes' walk from Raffles City MRT station, has lots of homeware shops. Chinatown has a mix of souvenir and antiques shops, including the very interesting People's Park Complex—still popular with locals—a good example of Singapore retailing circa the 1960s. In the colonial district try the lovely CHIJMES mall and nearby Raffles City for fashion and food. Antiques lovers should check out Tanglin Mall and the Paragon Shopping Centre. For an Indian department store experience, try Mustafa Centre in Serangoon Road, which opens 24 hours, every day of the year. While bargaining in the markets and suburban shops is considered part of the Singapore experience, and most electronic stores and jewelers will allow you to haggle a little, brand-name boutiques and department stores throughout Singapore have fixed and clearly marked prices.

As you would expect, retail is evolving in Singapore. Shopping has become such a lifestyle activity that destinations such as VivoCity and Marina Bay Sands meld entertainment with shopping in architectually stimulating surroundings. The Sunday flea market at the China Square Central Mall (Cross Street) is a little less polished, but for real old Singaporean charm head to the outdoor Thieves Market on Sungei Road. It's particularly festive after dark.

CONSUMER PROTECTION

Since Singaporeans and the 14 million annual visitors to the island take shopping seriously, the Singapore government is very keen to promote hassle-free, safe shopping for consumers. To aid and protect shoppers, the STB (Singapore Tourism Board) publishes a shopping guide (available at tourism offices) which lists good retailers—those preferred retailers chosen for their service and reliability—and a list of retailers to avoid. A special hotline number, 1800 736 2000, has been set up to assist tourists who have had bad retail experiences during their stay in Singapore. You can also email feedback@stb.com.sg.

Shopping by Theme

Whether you're looking for a department store, a quirky boutique, or something in between, you'll find it all in Singapore. On this page shops are listed by theme. For a more detailed write-up, see the individual listings in Singapore by Area.

ANTIQUES AND HANDICRAFTS

Antiques of the Orient (▷ 77)
Asiatique Collection (▷ 77)
Holland Road Shopping Centre (▷ 77)
Lim's Arts & Living (▷ 77)
Rumah Bebe (▷ 90)

BOOKS

Books Kinokuniya (▷ 36)

DEPARTMENT STORES

Mustafa Centre (▷ 47)
Tangs (▷ 47)
Yue Hwa Chinese Products Emporium (▷ 47)

EASTERN TRADING GOODS

Bangku Bangku (▷ 90)

ELECTRICAL AND ELECTRONIC GOODS

Funan Digitalife Mall (▷ 46)
Sim Lim Square (▷ 90

SHOPPING MALLS AND STREETS

313@Somerset (▷ 46)
Arab Street (▷ 41)
Bintan Mall (▷ 106)
Bugis Junction (▷ 90)
Bugis Street (▷ 41)
Centrepoint (▷ 46)
Chinatown Point (▷ 46)
Changi Village (▷ 90)
Clarke Quay(▷ 27)
Geylang Serai (▷ 90)
The Heeren (▷ 46)
112 Katong (▷ 90)
ION Orchard (▷ 46)
Johor Bahru Duty Free Complex (Zon) (▷ 106)
Lucky Plaza (▷ 46)
Mandarin Gallery (▷ 46)
Millenia Walk (▷ 46)
Orchard Central (▷ 47)
Orchard Road (▷ 36–37)
People's Park Complex (▷ 47)
Plaza Pelangi (▷ 106)
Raffles City (▷ 47)
Resorts World Sentosa Luxury Fashion Galleria (▷ 77)
Suntec City Mall (▷ 47)
Tanglin Mall (▷ 77)
Tanglin Shopping Centre (▷ 77)
Temple/Pagoda/Trengganu Streets (▷ 47)
Thieves Market (▷ 47)
VivoCity (▷ 77)

WATCHES AND JEWELRY

Terese Jade & Minerals (▷ 77)

Singapore by Night

There's plenty to do in Singapore at night. It's a safe city, too

Singapore is one of the world's great night cities, whether you want to shop, party or go on a safari.

Stepping Out

Retail stores remain open until 9 or 10pm daily (late shopping until 11pm every Saturday on Orchard Road), hawker food stands and restaurants provide fantastic choices of cuisine, and bars and clubs are often still packed into the early hours. Main areas to head to include Orchard Road (especially Emerald Hill); Boat, Robertson and Clarke quays; Chinatown (Ann Siang Hill); and the Colonial District (Marina Bay Sands). Around Bugis Street there's always some action, although the area is not as risqué as it was when it was the transsexual meeting place. Expats frequent Holland Village or the Orchard Road hotels.

Riverside Action

Arguably the best choice for those new to town is to head for Boat Quay or Clarke Quay (▷ 27) districts. Both areas have walkways, bars, clubs and restaurants to choose from, and a riverside nightlife ambience that is typically Singaporean. Alternatively, take an evening river cruise to get a different perspective of the city, with its old and new architecture and the night lights. Or head for one of the nightspots (▷ 48–49) for live or house music and a chance to party with the locals.

Fun Round the Clock

There is a glut of after-dark attractions in the city. It is now possible to go on a safari, play golf and make a bungee jump long after dusk.

DRINKING OUT

To get the night off to a good start, and to compensate for Singapore's noticeably high drink prices, take advantage of the happy hours that typically run from around 5pm until 8pm. Also, many places offer cheap or free drinks for women—check beforehand (▷ 48–49).

Eating Out

From such a vibrant and polyglot society you would expect an equally diverse range of food and restaurant choices, and Singapore does not disappoint.

Whether you want to eat a spicy dish wrapped in a banana leaf in a crowded, noisy food hall, or sit down in air-conditioned grandeur and dine on haute cuisine to the tinkling of a baby grand, Singapore offers you both choices and everything in between.

Culinary choices come from Malaysia, China, India and Indonesia, and "Singapore food" is a blend of all of these. Cantonese and Fijian cooking is prevalent, but so are the lesser-known food choices from Southern China, either prepared in stalls at steaming hawker centers where the occupants talk at rapid-fire speed, or in tiny Chinese restaurants tucked away in Chinatown.

Indian food is known the world over, but here you can try Malay Muslim or Indian Muslim fare. Known as "Mamak" food, you will know where to go to get this by looking for the restaurant signs written in Arabic.

For coffee, big brands like Starbucks and trendy cafés abound but Singapore's traditional coffee shops are no-nonsense, cheap and cheerful options for popular rice and noodle dishes, along with coffee that is thick and sweet.

HAND OR CUTLERY?

Many Hindus and Muslims eat their food with the right hand only; it is considered unclean to eat with the left hand, although it's okay to use utensils—usually a fork and spoon. Eating with your hand, you tear pieces of chapati (using only one hand) and then soak or scoop up elements of the meal. For rice there's another technique: you add the curries and work up the mixture into balls, which you then pick up and pop—almost flick—into your mouth.

Local cuisine is a fusion of Malaysian, Chinese, Indian and Indonesian

Restaurants by Cuisine

There are restaurants to suit all tastes and budgets in Singapore. On this page they are listed by cuisine. For a more detailed description of each restaurant, see Singapore by Area.

Top Tips For...

However you'd like to spend your time in Singapore, these top suggestions should help you tailor your ideal visit. Each sight or listing has a fuller write-up elsewhere in the book.

SAMPLING LOCAL CUISINE

Sample delicious Asian cuisines at Lau Pa Sat hawker centre (⊳ 31), in the business district, where you'll find a wide variety of Asian cuisines at super-low prices.

Indian food that is inexpensive and tasty, and eaten from a banana leaf, can be found at Komala Vilas (⊳ 51), in Little India.

Lau Pa Sat (top); crabs at Clarke Quay (above); Orchard Road street sign (below)

OUTDOOR DINING

Head south of Orchard Road to the Singapore River, where Clarke Quay (⊳ 27) has many riverside restaurants and bars.

Seafood lovers should head for Jumbo Seafood (⊳ 92). There, waterside walking trails will help you lose the pounds you put on over lunch.

ELECTRONIC GOODS

Go to Lucky Plaza (⊳ 46), on Orchard Road, to check out several levels of shops selling cameras, smartphones, tablets and other electricals.

For price comparisons and plenty of stores offering the latest gizmos and electronic wizardry at (almost) fixed prices, head for the Funan Digitalife Mall (⊳ 46).

BRAND-NAME CLOTHES

Start at upmarket Tangs (⊳ 47) and Resorts World Sentosa (⊳ 77), two of Singapore's top department stores.

The Shoppes at Marina Bay Sands (⊳ 34) has a mix of luxury international brands and emerging labels.

Designer shop on Orchard Road (right)

LEARNING ABOUT LOCAL CULTURE

Start at the National Museum of Singapore (▷ 35) then visit the nearby Asian Civilisations Museum (▷ 24–25) and the Singapore Art Museum (▷ 39).

Little India (▷ 32–33) is living culture, so wander around the main streets and back alleys and watch the locals go about their daily chores.

GOING OUT ON THE TOWN

Clarke Quay (▷ 27) offers a wide range of drinking, dining and nightclub options. Come here and join the expats in a beer.

Ready to kick back and dance the night away? Then head for Zouk (▷ 49), Singapore's most famous nightclub.

Singapore Art Museum (top); Clarke Quay (above); Little India (below)

STAYING AT BUDGET HOTELS

The holy grail in this pricey hotel city is good, clean accommodation that won't break the bank. YMCA International House (▷ 109), in Orchard Road, is an old favorite.

Prince of Wales (▷ 109), slap bang in the hustle and bustle of Little India, offers basic facilities along with a chill bar.

ENTERTAINING THE KIDS

Sentosa (▷ 62–63) will entertain the young ones for a day or more, with a cable-car ride, water park, beaches or trip to Universal Studios.

The Singapore Science Centre (▷ 68–69) has interactive exhibits on everything from climate change to DNA.

Singapore Science Centre Human Anatomy section (left)

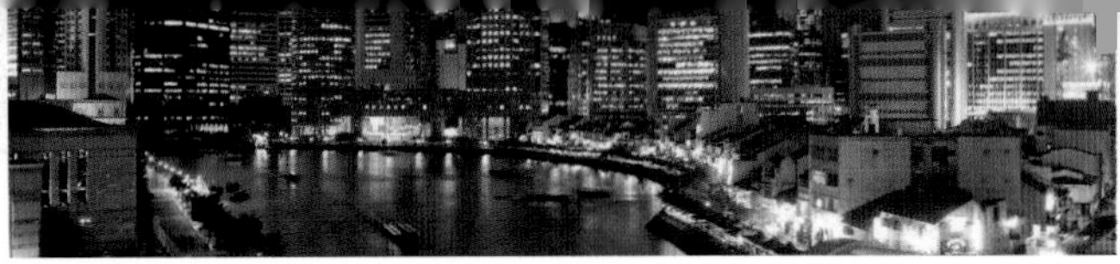

The Post Bar (below); Bukit Timah (middle)

A POSH NIGHT OUT

The stylish Post Bar at the Fullerton Hotel (▷ 49) serves a wide selection of classic cocktails in elegant surroundings.

The highest rooftop bar in Singapore, the alfresco gastrobar 1 Altitude (▷ 48) is an essential big-night warm-up.

A WALK ON THE WILD SIDE

Start early or late to avoid the midday heat for a walk along the trails of Bukit Timah (▷ 66), a patch of primary tropical rainforest within reach of the city center.

Singapore's only protected wetland, the 320-acre (130-hectare) Sungei Buloh Wetland Reserve (▷ 67), is home to over 500 species of tropical flora and fauna.

THRILL SEEKING

A pair of adrenaline attractions at Clarke Quay (▷ 27) are the G-Max Reverse Bungee and the GX-5, which allows five riders to freefall and swing out across the Singapore River.

Buzz down the 700yd/m Skyline Luge toboggan run, ride a wave at Wave House or try indoor sky-diving at Sentosa (▷ 62–63).

Esplanade concert hall roof (above); ostrich at Jurong Bird Park (below)

BIRDS AND ANIMALS

One of the world's best places to view tropical birds is at Jurong Bird Park (▷ 58–59), where almost 400 species are kept in aviaries and walk-through enclosures.

Seeing nocturnal animals at a time when they are active is made easy and informative by a ride on the tram at the Night Safari (▷ 60–61).

Singapore by Area

The City

Immerse yourself in the galleries of world-class museums, stroll the vibrant streets and back lanes of Chinatown, or take a walk down Orchard Road.

2
3
4
5
6
7
8
C
D
E
0
250 m
250 yds
Shrewsbury Road
(CTE)
EXPRESSWAY
THOMSON ROAD
United Square
Surrey Road
Hon Clan Temple
Dernish Road
NEWTON ROAD
Lincoln Road
Wee Nam Road
HAMPSHIRE BRIDGE
CENTRAL
Norfolk
Carlisle
Cambridge Road
Truro Road
Owen Road
KENG LEE ROAD
KAMPONG JAVA ROAD
Hertford Road
Bristol Road
Dorset Road
Newton Circus
Newton
BUKIT TIMAH ROAD
Monk's Hill Terrace
Hooper Rd
Cavenagh
Rutland Road
Swimming Complex
DORSET BRIDGE
Kampong Java Park
Hampshire Road
CLEMENCEAU AVENUE
Winstedt Road
Monk's Hill Road
SCOTTS ROAD
Anthony Road
Peck Hay Road
Cairnhill Road
Cairnhill Rise
Istana Presidential Palace
Free Church of Singapore
Little India
Buffalo Rd
The Verge
American Club
Shaw Centre
Lido
CAIRNHILL CIRCLE
Elizabeth
Nutmeg Road
Mount Elizabeth
Istana Park
Mackenzie Road
Mount Emily Park
Mount Emily Road
Academy of Fine Arts
Upper Wilkie Road
Wilkie Road
Church of Christ of Malaya
Niven Road
ORCHARD ROAD
Orchard
Orchard Turn
The Paragon
BIDEFORD ROAD
CAIRNHILL ROAD
Al-Falah Mosque
Saunders Road
Hullet Road
Emerald Hill Road
Starhub Centre
Sri Temasek
CITY
Sophia Road
Mount Sophia
SELEGIE ROAD
Orchard Road
The Hereen
Mandarin Arcade
Faber House
Centrepoint
Cavenagh Road
Kramat Road
Kramat Lane
Buyong Rd
Edinburgh Road
Adis Road
Peace Centre
Orchard Link
Orchard Cineleisure
BOULEVARD
SOMERSET ROAD
Somerset
Oldham Lane
Dhoby Ghaut
Handy Road
Bencoolen Mosque
Prinsep St
PRINSEP ST
GRANGE ROAD
EXETER ROAD
EBER ROAD
PENANG ROAD
Comcentre
Devonshire Road
Tiverton Lane
House of Tan Yeok Nee
Presbyterian Church
Penang Lane
Park Mall
Singapore Art Museum
Leonie Hill Road
Thomas Walk
Saint Thomas Walk
Killiney
Lloyd Road
Oxley Road
Chesed-El Synagogue
OXLEY RISE
FORT CANNING RD
National Museum of Singapore
Cathedral of the Good Shepherd
Church of the Sacred Heart
Oxley Walk
Fort Canning Park
Cox Terrace
Asian Sculpture Garden
Canning Rise
STAMFORD
RIVER VALLEY ROAD
Sri Thandayuthapani Temple (Chettiar's Temple)
Tank Road
AVENUE
Fort Canning Service Reservoir
National Archives
Peranakan Museum
River Valley Close
Singapore Buddhist Lodge
Kim Yam Road
Tong Watt Road
KIM SENG BRIDGE
Unity Street
Merbau Road
G-Max Reverse Bungee & GX5
St Gregory's Armenian Church
Funan IT Mall
Kim Seng Road
Jiak Kim Street
Martin Road
Robertson Quay
Rodyk Street
Saiboo Street
Mohamed Sultan Road
Nanson Road
Clarke Quay
Clarke St
North Boat Quay
HILL ST
HIGH ST
High Street Centre
CLEMENCEAU BRIDGE
Tan Si Chong Su Temple
Singapore
COLEMAN BRIDGE
Parliament House
HAVELOCK ROAD
Outram Road
READ BRIDGE
Boat Quay
Merchant Rd
Riverwalk Galleria
ELGIN BRIDGE
CLEMENCEAU
Magazine Rd
Melaka Mosque
New Market Rd
Carpenter Street
Hongkong St
Circular Rd
Singapore River
Jalan Minyak
York Hill
CENTRAL EXPRESSWAY (CTE)
Manhattan House
HAVELOCK ROAD
EU TONG SEN STREET
North Canal Road
Hong Lim Park
Havelock Square
UPPER CROSS ST
People's Park Centre
Pearl's Hill Terrace
Pearl's Hill City Park
Upper Hokien St
PICKERING
Pidemco Centre
South Canal Rd
Yueh Hai Ching Temple
Pearl's Hill Reservoir
People's Park Complex
Chinatown
Chinatown Point
Hokien St
CROSS STREET
CHURCH STREET
Phillip St
Outram Park
CHINATOWN
Sri Mariamman Temple
Pagoda St
Temple St
Smith St
Jamae Mosque
Club St
Fuk Tak Chi Museum
1B
OUTRAM FLYOVER
OUTRAM
Pearl Bank Apartment
Pearl Bank
College Road
Third Hospital Avenue
Oriental Plaza
Kreta Ayer People's Theatre
Trengganu St
SOUTH
BRIDGE
Nagore Durgha
Telok Ayer
Boon Tat Street
Amoy St
City House
Pearl's Centre
Singapore General Hospital
Second Hospital Avenue
First Hospital Ave
Outram Park
Buddha Tooth Relic Temple
Keong Saik Rd
Teck Lim Rd
Duxton Plain Park
Ann Siang Rd
Thain Hock Keng Temple
Stanley Street
McCallum St
Red Dot Museum
ROAD
NEW BRIDGE ROAD
St Matthew's Church
Bukit Pasoh Rd
NEIL ROAD
Duxton Hill
Duxton Road
TANJONG PAGAR ROAD
MAXWELL ROAD
CECIL STREET
ROBINSON ROAD
SHENTON WAY
White House
Craig Road
Everton Park
CANTONMENT ROAD
Phoo Thor Chi Temple
Wallich Street
Tanjong Pagar
Tras Street
Peck Seah Street
Choon Guan St
Temasek Tower
Singapore Conference Hall
Seng Wong Beo Temple
Prince Edward Road
Yan Kit Road
Realty Centre
Enggor Street
ANSON ROAD
Anson Centre
Hock Teck See Temple
Hoe Chiang Rd
Cantonment Link
Palmer Road

The City

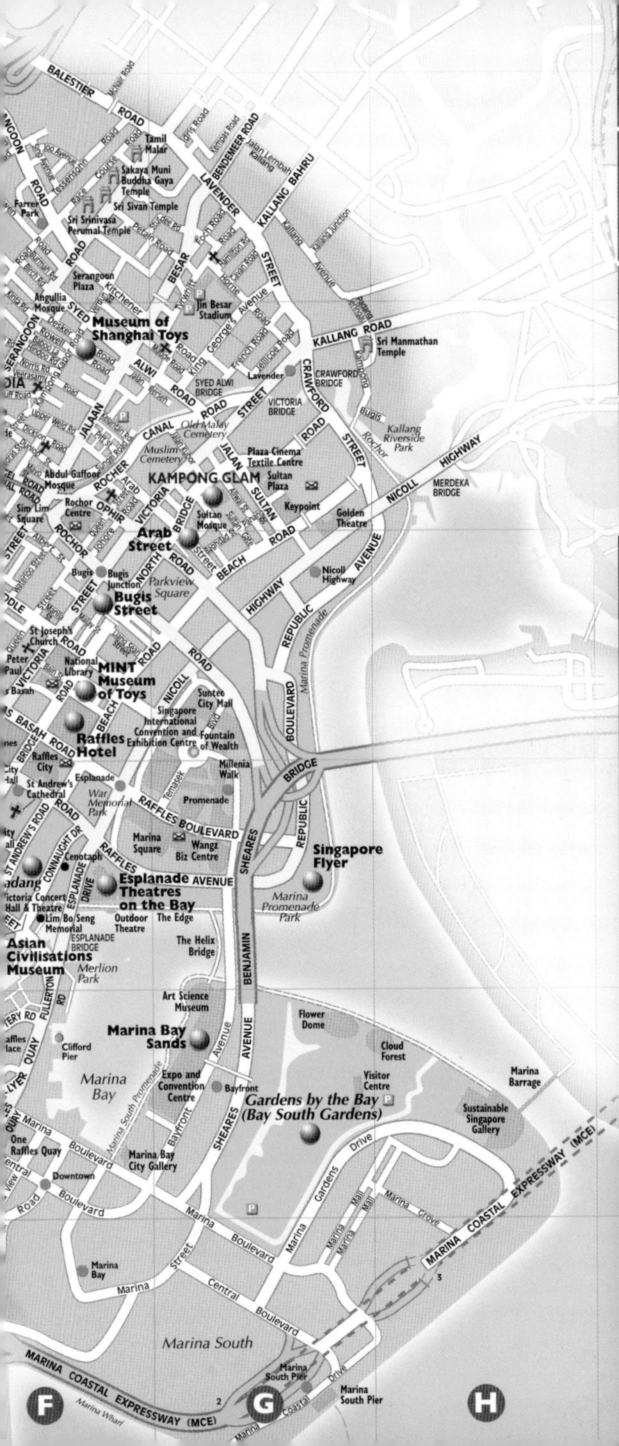
BALESTIER ROAD
McNair Road
Tamil Malar
Sakaya Muni Buddha Gaya Temple
Sri Sivan Temple
Sri Srinivasa Perumal Temple
Farrer Park
Race Course Road
Tessensohn
Petain Road
Serangoon Plaza
Kitchener
Angullia Mosque
SYED ALWI
Museum of Shanghai Toys
Jin Besar Stadium
LAVENDER
BESAR
BENDEMEER ROAD
Jalan Lembah Kallang
KALLANG BAHRU
Kallang Avenue
Kallang Junction
Tyrwhitt
Horne
Foch Road
Hamilton Rd
Cavan Road
King George's Avenue
French Road
Jellicoe Road
Lavender
KALLANG ROAD
Sri Manmathan Temple
CRAWFORD BRIDGE
CRAWFORD STREET
SYED ALWI BRIDGE
VICTORIA BRIDGE
ALWI ROAD
JALAN BESAR
CANAL ROAD
Old Malay Cemetery
Muslim Cemetery
JALAAN
ROCHOR
Abdul Gaffoor Mosque
Rochor Centre
Sim Lim Square
OPHIR ROAD
KAMPONG GLAM
Plaza Cinema
Textile Centre
Sultan Plaza
Keypoint
Sultan Mosque
Golden Theatre
Kallang Riverside Park
Bugis
Rochor
NICOLL HIGHWAY
MERDEKA BRIDGE
Arab Street
NORTH BRIDGE ROAD
BEACH ROAD
Nicoll Highway
Parkview Square
Bugis Junction
Bugis Street
HIGHWAY
REPUBLIC BOULEVARD
Marina Promenade
St Joseph's Church
National Library
MINT Museum of Toys
Raffles Hotel
Suntec City Mall
Singapore International Convention and Exhibition Centre
Fountain of Wealth
Millenia Walk
BRIDGE
Raffles City
Esplanade
St Andrew's Cathedral
War Memorial Park
Temasek
Promenade
RAFFLES BOULEVARD
Marina Square
Wangz Biz Centre
SHEARES
Singapore Flyer
Cenotaph
CONNAUGHT DR
ESPLANADE DRIVE
Esplanade Theatres on the Bay
RAFFLES AVENUE
Marina Promenade Park
Victoria Concert Hall & Theatre
Lim Bo Seng Memorial
Outdoor Theatre
The Edge
The Helix Bridge
ESPLANADE BRIDGE
Asian Civilisations Museum
Merlion Park
BENJAMIN
FULLERTON RD
Art Science Museum
Flower Dome
Cloud Forest
Marina Bay Sands
Clifford Pier
AVENUE
Marina Bay
Expo and Convention Centre
Bayfront
Visitor Centre
Marina Barrage
Gardens by the Bay (Bay South Gardens)
Sustainable Singapore Gallery
Marina South Promenade
One Raffles Quay
Marina Boulevard
Marina Bay City Gallery
Downtown
Marina Gardens Drive
Marina Mall
Marina Grove
MARINA COASTAL EXPRESSWAY (MCE)
Marina Street
Central Boulevard
Marina Bay
Marina South
Marina South Pier
Marina Wharf
Marina Coastal Drive
F
G
H
2
3

Asian Civilisations Museum

TOP 25

HIGHLIGHTS

- Chinese history timeline
- Red bat motifs
- Buddhist statues
- Literati gallery
- Jade collection
- Qing Dynasty porcelain
- Kang tables
- Islamic collection

TIP

- Guided tours, given several times a day, are the perfect way to learn more about Asian culture.

Displaying relics of mainland China, continental India, Islamic West Asia and Southeast Asian cultures, this excellent museum is housed in a gorgeous colonial waterfront building.

Scene setter The imposing 1865 Empress Place building sets the stage for a fascinating look at the artistic, cultural and religious developments of Asia. The continent has been cleverly divided into four distinct regions—China, Southeast Asia, West Asia (the Islamic world) and the Indian subcontinent. Like the National Museum of Singapore (▷ 35) and the prestigious Singapore Art Museum (▷ 39), this museum is managed by Singapore's National Heritage Board. Special exhibitions further explore the cultures of these parts of the world.

Clockwise from left: a sandstone figure of Buddha (Cambodia, 11th–12th century); a Chinese porcelain Buddha; the museum exterior; a Kraak dish showing two Persian ladies of the Safavid period; Lakhoun Khaol dance mask from Cambodia and a gamelan display

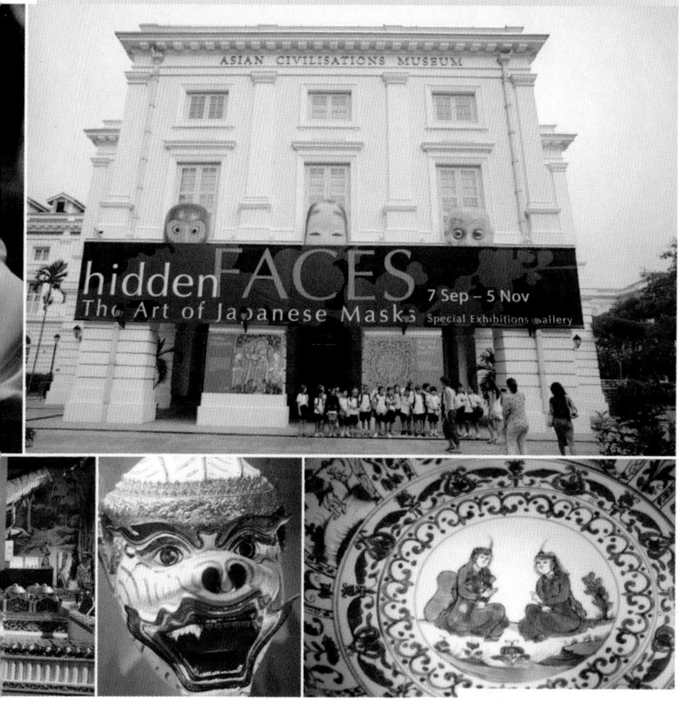

Multimedia There are a total of 11 theme galleries spread over three levels, displaying artifacts that represent a microcosm of Asian civilizations.

The story of Asia is showcased with displays, interactive exhibits and multimedia presentations to help you learn more about the multifaceted aspects of Asian cultures.

The Singapore River Gallery tells many stories, of Chinese "coolies," indigenous Orang Laut from Malaya and the more recently arrived Europeans. The West Asia Gallery explains the importance of the mosque in Islamic societies. The Southeast Asia Gallery is full of lavish textile exhibits, while the China Gallery has a fascinating "interview with the Emperor" video display, and a stunning life-size example of the Son of Heaven's yellow ceremonial robe.

THE BASICS

www.acm.org.sg
F6
1 Empress Place
6332 7798
Mon 1–7, Tue–Sun 9–7 (Fri until 9)
Indochine Waterfront Restaurant; bar; café
Raffles Place
75, 100, 130, 131, 167
Good
Moderate
Free guided tours Mon 2, Tue–Fri 11, 2; Sat, Sun 11, 2, 3, 4. Museum shops. Temporary exhibitions

Chinatown

TOP 25

Detail from Thin Hock Keng Temple (left); shop façades (middle); outside Thain Hock Keng Temple (right)

THE BASICS

E7
South Bridge Road and surrounding streets
Smith Street
Chinatown
2, 5, 12, 33, 51, 61, 62, 63, 81, 84, 103, 104, 124, 143, 145, 147, 166, 174, 181, 190, 197, 520, 851
None
Free

HIGHLIGHTS

- Maxwell Road Food Centre
- Ann Siang Hill
- Chinese shophouses
- Buddha Tooth Relic Temple
- Chinatown Heritage Centre

TIP

- Come prepared for lots of walking as you'll be tempted to check out interesting backstreets.

The best time to visit is just before Chinese New Year, when the streets throb and vibrant stands sell everything from waxed ducks to *hong bao*, red packets for giving money as presents.

Singapore's Chinatown This area covers the streets leading off South Bridge Road between Maxwell Road and the Singapore River. As a policy, conservation of the old buildings goes hand-in-hand with new development here, and though better than destruction, the often rather cosmetic results and years of unsympathetic infilling have left only a few streets with the authentic atmosphere and activities of old Chinatown.

What to see Erskine Road and Ann Siang Hill exhibit some of the best efforts of preservation. Temple and Trengganu streets have many traditional shophouses and coffee shops, while Pagoda Street, similar in character, also has the Chinatown Heritage Centre. Nearby Smith Street is the area's appointed "food alley", with lots of covered outdoor eating options. South Bridge Road, between Upper Cross Street and Maxwell Road, is home to fascinating places of worship. Telok Ayer Street, although much renovated, is also worth a visit. Thian Hock Keng Temple (the Temple of Heavenly Happiness) is the oldest Chinese temple in the city. The newest addition is Buddha Tooth Relic Temple, father along South Bridge Road. The imperious building, opened in 2007, was designed as a mixture of Tang dynasty palace and traditional Buddhist mandala.

Riverside Point shopping mall (left); chefs preparing food in one of Clarke Quay's many restaurants (right)

TOP 25

Clarke Quay

Like Singapore's food options, the range of nightlife venues has grown so large that it's difficult to pick the best. But, for its scenic—and central—location, the renovated Clarke Quay is tough to beat.

Working quay Just upriver from the marina and the Raffles landing site, Clarke Quay was at the heart of the 19th-century trade route through Singapore. As recently as the 1980s, this riverside strand was a hive of maritime entrepreneurialism.

Revival These days the whole quay area is owned by one of Asia's biggest real estate companies, who gave it a multimillion-dollar facelift. Five art deco godowns (blocks of warehouses) have been refurbished in pastel hues, but the historic grandeur has been given a modern finish thanks to a climate-control canopy. Smaller lampshade covers line the riverfront and make it possible to sit out by the water without being bothered by the heat. In total, there are 62 eating, entertainment, drinking, retail and lifestyle outlets, including some essential night stops: The Arena for live music and the Pump Room bar. It's a must-visit for tourists, but part of the attraction is that it's a party spot also loved by locals.

Thrill rides The latest addition to Clarke Quay is a pair of adrenaline-pumping rides—the G-Max Reverse Bungee and GX-5 Extreme Swing. The former pings riders skyward at speed, the other is a giant swing that arcs out across the Singapore River at speeds up to 75mph (120kph).

THE BASICS

www.clarkequay.com.sg
E6
3 River Valley Road
6337 3292
24 hours
Various
Clarke Quay
Generally good
Individual venues may charge a cover

HIGHLIGHTS

- Reverse Bungee and GX-5 Swing
- Indochine restaurant

Gardens by the Bay

TOP 25

HIGHLIGHTS

- Flower Dome
- Cloud Forest
- Supertree Grove
- Heritage Gardens
- The Meadow

Just a short walk from the Central Business District, this 250-acre (100-hectare) complex—split into three waterfront spaces—brings even more green to the already lush and tropical city.

Bay South This is the section of the park where you will find the futuristic grove of Supertrees. The 16-story-tall vertical gardens have been designed to collect rainwater, generate solar power and act as venting ducts for the park's conservatories. Schedule in a walk along the OCBC Skyway, a 140yd/m walkway between two Supertrees. This is where you'll gain a bird's-eye view of the entire landscape. Nearby you'll find The Meadow, Singapore's largest outdoor garden venue, hosting tons of big events and outdoor concerts.

Clockwise from left: the alien-looking Supertrees are fitted with state-of-the-art technology that mimics the ecological function of real trees; aerial view of Gardens By the Bay in the shadow of neighboring Marina Bay Sands resort; refreshing waterfall in the Cloud Forest conservatory

Hothouses Tropical trees and blossoms set the scene for a great evening stroll along the waterfront promenade, or beat the heat with a trip inside one of the two armadillo-shaped conservatories. The Cloud Forest has the world's largest indoor waterfall and the Flower Dome hosts plants from the Mediterranean and semi-arid subtropical regions.

Dining in the park A variety of dining options are available at Gardens by the Bay. Pollen, set up in the Flower Dome and helmed by renowned chef Jason Atherton, offers Mediterranean-influenced, modern European cuisine. If you prefer a more casual setting, try Satay by the Bay or head up high to the Supertree Dining for everything from noodles and fast-food options to Singapore staples.

THE BASICS

www.gardensbythebay.com.sg
G7
10 Marina Gardens Drive
6420 6848
Outdoor gardens daily 5am–2am; conservatories and OCBC Skyway daily 9–9
Various
Bayfront
Generally good
Conservatories expensive

Kampong Glam

TOP 25

Sultan Mosque (left); at prayer in the mosque (middle) and pashminas on sale (right)

THE BASICS

Sultan Mosque
G4
3 Muscat Street
6293 4405
Daily 11–7
Numerous coffee shops
Bugis
2, 32, 51, 61, 63, 84, 133, 145, 197
None
Free

HIGHLIGHTS

- Bussorah Street
- Gilded dome of Sultan Mosque
- Prayer hall
- Istana Kampong Glam
- Murtabak
- Batik
- Haji Lane
- Malay Heritage Centre

The golden domes and minarets of Sultan Mosque, glinting in the late-afternoon sun, and the call of the *muezzin*, remind you that this area of Singapore is very much part of the Islamic world.

In the past Kampong Glam, where the Sultan of Singapore lived, was set aside in the early days for Malay, Arab and Bugis (Sulawesi) traders. The "Glam" may be named after the *gelam* tree from which medicinal oil was produced.

Today Although there are many mosques on the island, Sultan Mosque is the focus of worship for Singapore's Muslim (mainly Malay) community. There has been a mosque on this site since 1824, when the East India Company made a grant for its construction. The present mosque dates from 1928, and reveals an interesting mix of Middle Eastern and Moorish influences. Its gilded dome is impressive; unusually, its base is made from bottles. Seen as you walk up Bussorah Street, with its shophouses at the rear, the mosque is truly stunning. Visitors are welcome outside prayer times, as long as they are well covered—no shorts. The *istana* (palace), built in the 1840s, is at the top of Sultan Gate and houses the Malay Heritage Centre. The surrounding streets are filled with a mix of shops selling souk items like basketware, perfume and carpets, and trendy independent boutiques offering the latest fashions. Come nighttime, the area's Muslim coffee shops, shisha cafés, cocktail bars and music lounges are all bustling.

The entrance to the market (left); the magnificent interior (right)

TOP 25

Lau Pa Sat

Choosing the best place to enjoy Singapore's legendary street food may seem futile, such are the options. However, if you only make it to one hawker food center, make it this one.

Setting Lau Pa Sat's appeal is as much about architecture and accessibility as it is about good food. Located at the point where Chinatown and the glitzy Central Business District (CBD) collide, the food area is housed within the largest remaining Victorian cast-iron building in Asia. It was built in 1894 on the site of an earlier outdoor wet market (the name means "old market" in Hokkien) and, even after a S$4 million renovation completed in 2014, remains a magnificently ornate structure. Columns and embellished arches hold up the gazebo from which ceiling fans hang, the clock tower chimes on the hour, and the forecourt teems to the sound of cooking and feasting.

Nighttime By day Lau Pa Sat caters to the office crowd from the CBD but has more local color by night. The more than 100 food stalls range from Malay through Indian to Chinese. However, satay snacks remain the most popular specialty. Boon Tat Street, alongside, is closed to traffic in the evenings when pushcarts hawking satay, *teh tarik* (hand-pulled milk tea), barbequed meats and seafood line the street. Back in the main building itself, there is a great dessert and drink counter where you can buy Singapore's famed ice-snacks. The food, as at all of the hawker centers, is very cheap and all tables are communal.

THE BASICS

- F7
- 18 Raffles Quay
- 24 hours
- Chinatown Food Street is on Smith Street, just north of the temple
- Raffles Place. Walk toward Robinson Road
- Several small steps
- Free

HIGHLIGHTS

- Boon Tat Street
- Hainan Chicken Rice
- Laksa
- Sago topped ice desserts

TIP

- Though it's open 24 hours, this isn't the best late-night hawker hub in Singapore. Try to visit between 6pm and 8pm.

Little India

TOP 25

HIGHLIGHTS

- Sari shops
- Banana-leaf meals
- Fish-head curry
- Perfumed garlands
- Fortune-tellers
- Temples
- Spice shops

TIP

- The district comes alive with throngs of Singapore's Indian guest workers on Sundays.

Along Serangoon Road and the streets that surround it you can snatch all the sensations of India. Exotic aromas fill the air. Baskets overflow with spices. Stores are packed with colorful cloth.

Origins of Little India In the mid-19th century, lime pits and brick kilns were set up in the area, and it is thought that these attracted Singapore's Indians, who were laborers for the most part, to Serangoon Road. The swampy grasslands here were also good for raising cattle, another traditional occupation of the Indian community.

Little India today The district remains overwhelmingly Indian, full of sari-clad women, spice shops, jasmine-garland sellers, Hindu

Clockwise from left: garland stall on Serangoon Road; banana leaf curry; browsing the shop stalls; gold shop on Serangoon Road; window shutters with garlands; Sri Veeramakaliamman Temple

temples and restaurants. Apart from the lively streets and tempting food emporiums, there is also the Tekka (Zhujiao) Centre at the southern end of Serangoon Road, which has an excellent food center on the ground floor and clothes shops above. Across from the market, a little way up Serangoon Road, Komala Vilas restaurant (▷ 51) serves wonderful *dosai* (savory pancakes) and *thali* (mixed curries)—all vegetarian—as well as delicious Indian sweets. Walk along Serangoon Road and you will come to Sri Veeramakaliamman Temple, dedicated to the ferocious goddess Kali. Farther on still is the Sri Srinivasa Perumal Temple, with its magnificent 1979 *gopuram* (ornamental gateway). Take a detour to Race Course Lane for a selection of banana-leaf restaurants offering fish-head curry.

THE BASICS

www.littleindia.com.sg
F4
Serangoon Road
Many restaurants and cafés
Little India, Farrer Park
8, 13, 20, 23, 26, 31, 64, 65, 66, 67, 81, 90, 97, 103, 106, 111, 125, 131, 133, 139, 142, 147, 151, 154, 865
Free

Marina Bay Sands' three hotel towers are each 55 stories high

Marina Bay Sands

TOP 25

THE BASICS

www.marinabaysands.com
G7
10 Bayfront Avenue
6688 8868
Shoppes mall daily 10am–11pm (varies between shops); ArtScience Museum daily 10–7
Various
Bayfront
ArtScience Museum
ArtScience Museum expensive

HIGHLIGHTS

- Celebrity restaurants
- Casino
- ArtScience Museum
- SkyPark
- The Shoppes at Marina Bay Sands
- Malay Heritage Centre

Resembling a surfboard sitting atop three high-rise buildings, this integrated resort immediately became an iconic part of the Singapore skyline when it opened in 2010.

Architectural masterpiece Israeli architect Moshe Safdie was inspired by the shape of a deck of cards when he designed the three towers, along with the ArtScience Museum, the shopping mall and casino. Feng shui consultants were brought in to ensure that everything met Eastern standards as well.

View from above Sands SkyPark on the 57th floor offers a 360-degree view of the skyline. Here you will find Sky on 57 restaurant and Ku Dé Ta bar, and guests of Marina Bay Sands hotel can take a dip in the infinity pool.

ArtScience Museum This lotus-shaped building is incorporated into a laser light show every night, but the star attractions are inside. The 21 galleries celebrate creativity in all fields and have hosted touring exhibitions such as Lego sensation Nathan Saway's "The Art of the Brick".

Inside the mall In addition to hosting over 300 stores, including big name brands like Prada and Louis Vuitton, the Shoppes at Marina Bay Sands complex is home to several celebrity chefs, including Mario Batali and Daniel Boulud. Near these top dining options, you'll find two state-of-the-art theaters which have hosted huge hits such as *Wicked* and *The Lion King*.

The museum is housed in a colonial building (left); exhibits in the film gallery (right)

National Museum of Singapore

TOP 25

Originally opened at the Raffles Museum and Library in 1887, this palatial structure has been transformed into one of Asia's truly great museums with a fantastic multimedia history exhibition.

Revamped Reopened in December 2006 after a major renovation, the former Singapore History Museum is a must-visit destination. The appeal goes beyond the sumptuous colonial building and expertly curated exhibitions. The real reason to visit is the Singapore History Gallery where the country's past sparks to life.

History gallery Singapore's documented history may be brief, but it is never boring. Precolonial history is dispensed within a single gallery, which includes the Singapore Stone, a lump of 1,000-year-old rock inscribed with a language that has never been deciphered. Then visitors are asked to choose between two pathways through the museum. One tells Singapore's story from the point of view of Everyman, the other introduces the characters who have shaped the nation's development. Both are fascinating.

The accompanying audio guide is key. By punching the numbers written on the museum floor into the gadget, visitors drive forward the narrative. The audio sometimes offers extra information, but there are also dramatizations of important scenes, or commentaries. The four lifestyle galleries are incredibly interactive and feature pared-down exhibitions on food, photography, fashion and film.

THE BASICS

www.nationalmuseum.sg
E5
93 Stamford Road
6332 3659
History Gallery: daily 10–6 (last admission 5.30). Living Galleries: daily 10–8 (last entry 7.30)
Fine dining restaurants and an all-day café
Bras Basah 5 min. Dhoby Ghaut 5 min
Many, including 7, 14, 16 and 36
Good
Moderate
Free English-language tours of the history gallery on some days

HIGHLIGHTS

- Singapore History Gallery
- The Singapore Stone
- Personal testimony from POWs interned by Japan
- Exhibition of Asia's herbs and spices in the Food Gallery

Orchard Road

TOP 25

HIGHLIGHTS

- Specialist shops
- Exclusive designer shops
- Coffee shops
- Centrepoint
- Books Kinokuniya
- Takashimaya
- ION Orchard
- Orchard Central
- Mandarin Gallery

TIP

- Don't be tempted to jaywalk on this long road; look for the underground crossing points.

One of the world's great shopping boulevards, Orchard Road is the retail heart and soul of Singapore. Day or night, a stroll from one end to the other is a pleasure, even if you don't shop.

Room to move Wide sidewalks and plenty of potential coffee stops help make encountering the cosmopolitan charms of Orchard Road a pleasure. And escaping the extreme heat that this equatorial city experiences is as easy as dashing into one of the dozens of air-conditioned shopping malls that line the street. Goods from all parts of the world are on offer, including well-priced electrical items, designer fashions, antiques and gifts. Inexpensive food courts are prevalent and there are any number of good restaurants. For a fine walking tour, start at Centrepoint, near

Clockwise from left: Louis Vuitton store; ladies' fashion on display; Heeren Junction; Paragon Shopping Mall; ION Orchard

Somerset Station, and walk to Tanglin Mall at the western end of the street. On the way, pause near the intersection with Scotts Road to drop in at ION Orchard, or take in a film at the nearby Lido Cineplex.

Mall heaven While the first malls appeared along this shopping drag in the 1970s, it's been non-stop development ever since, with the latest major revamp in 2009. This was when ION Orchard was added, with its curvaceous futuristic design, observation deck, media facade and 300-plus shops. Orchard Central, which is the same age, holds the title of "tallest vertical mall" with 14 floors of retail space, including two below ground level. The four-level Mandarin Gallery is another retail haven, hosting top international brands such as Bathing Ape, Y-3 and Marc by Marc Jacobs.

THE BASICS

www.orchardroad.org
C4/D5/E5
Restaurants, food courts, supermarket
Orchard, Somerset
7, 14, 16, 65, 106, 111, 123, 167, 605
Good

Raffles Hotel

TOP 25

Raffles Hotel exterior (left); the famous Singapore Sling (middle) and the courtyard (right)

THE BASICS

www.raffleshotel.com
F5
1 Beach Road
6337 1886
2 cafés, bakery, Chinese restaurant, grill, Tiffin room, deli and "fusion" restaurant
City Hall
14, 16, 36, 56, 82, 100, 107, 125, 167
Good

HIGHLIGHTS

- Front facade
- Lobby
- Tiffin Room
- Bar and Billiard Room
- Singapore Sling
- Palm Court
- Long Bar

The renovators may have tried too hard—the Long Bar, for instance, was repositioned to allow for a two-story bar to cater to the hordes of visitors—but Raffles remains one of the world's great heritage hotels.

Legend Say "Raffles" and you might conjure up an image of the very epitome of colonial style and service. Established by the Sarkies brothers in 1887, the hotel served the traders and travelers who, after the opening of the Suez Canal in 1869, were visiting the bustling commercial hub of Singapore in growing numbers. Over the years guests have included Somerset Maugham, Elizabeth Taylor, Noël Coward, Michael Jackson and Rudyard Kipling.

Renowned establishment Within just a decade of opening, the original 10-room bungalow had been expanded and the two-story wings added. The main building was opened in 1899. Over the years the Raffles Hotel has acquired a worldwide reputation for fine service and food, with its charming blend of classical architecture and tropical gardens. The elegant Raffles Courtyard is at the back of the main building.

Other facilities The Jubilee Hall is a charming Victorian-style theater that hosts all sorts of ceremonies and events throughout the year. Some 70 specialist shops adjoin the main building, including one dedicated to selling Raffles memorabilia.

The Art Museum exterior (left); some of the items on display (middle and right)

TOP 25

Singapore Art Museum

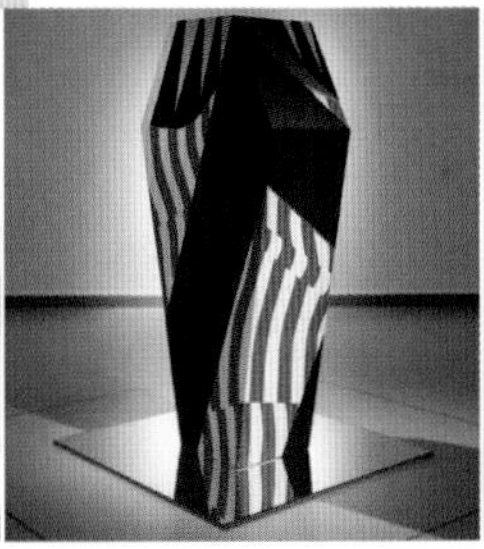

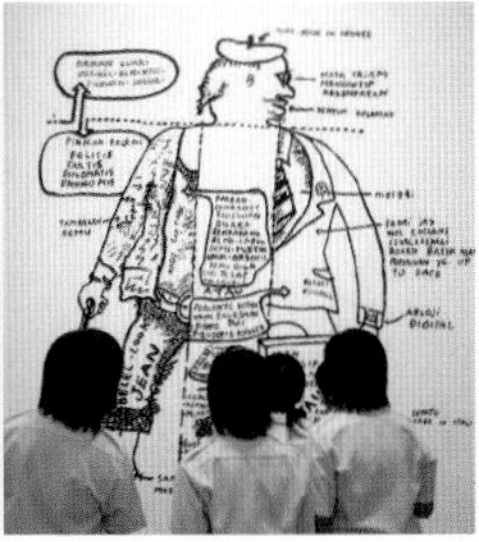

With its focus on art of the 20th century, this is Singapore's flagship art museum dedicated to the collection and display of contemporary works from Singapore and Southeast Asia. It also presents traveling exhibitions.

National treasure The museum, opened in 1996, is housed in the restored 19th-century St. Joseph's Institution building, a former Catholic boys' school, and displays Singapore's national art collection. The permanent collection has grown from less than 2,000 artworks to more than 10,000, and now houses the largest and most comprehensive collection of 20th-century Southeast Asian art in the region.

State of the art Almost 107,600sq ft (10,000sq m) of floor space includes 14 galleries, a reference library, an auditorium, a multipurpose hall, a museum shop, courtyards and an electronic E-image Gallery that runs interactive programs featuring some of the museum's collection on a large visual monitor. Check out Museum Label SAM at 8Q, a museum extension round the corner at 8 Queen Street, displaying a selection of multidisciplinary and interactive works.

On show An overview of Singaporean art is on permanent display and traveling exhibitions expose the region internationally. A community program covers a diversity of art trends and practices, fringe activities and lectures.

THE BASICS

www.singaporeartmuseum.sg

- F5
- 71 Bras Basah Road
- 6332 3222
- Daily 10–7 (Fri 10–9)
- Café adjacent
- Dhoby Ghaut, Bras Basah
- 14, 16, 36, 77, 124, 131, 162, 174
- Few
- Moderate; free admission Fri 6–9 and Mon–Fri 12–2
- Free guided tours Tue–Fri 11, 2, Sat, Sun 11, 2, 3.30. Museum shop

HIGHLIGHTS

- 19th-century building
- Large collection
- E-image Gallery
- Library
- Museum
- Temporary exhibitions

Singapore Flyer

TOP 25

The observation wheel (left); view from one of the cabins (right)

THE BASICS

www.singaporeflyer.com.sg
G6
30 Raffles Avenue
6734 8829
Daily 8.30am–10.30pm
Seafood, steak, Mexican, Japanese, among others
Promenade
Good
Expensive
The security procedures are similar to an airport, and it's best to allow up to 30 min to collect tickets and pass through the check-points. For an extra S$40, you can enjoy a cocktail during your flight

HIGHLIGHTS

- Views as far as Malaysia and Indonesia on clear days
- Singapore's sparkling nighttime skyline

Opened to great fanfare in spring 2008, the world's largest observation wheel offers a spectacular perspective on the urban heart of Singapore, with Malaysia and Indonesia also visible on clear days.

Orientation Perched on the edge of the Marina, and climbing to an impressive 541ft (165m), the Singapore Flyer is 100ft (30m) taller than the London Eye and a prominent feature on the skyline. The ever-changing perspective and pedestrian speed make it a great way to familiarize yourself with the layout of the shiny new Marina Bay Sands development below.

Panoramic views The ride lasts around 35 minutes and begins with views back across the Marina to the skyscrapers of the Central Business District. This angle also offers a great overview of the impressive Marina Bay Sands architecture (▷ 34). The comedown focuses attention on the north of the city, taking in Kampong Glam, Little India and the northeastern districts of Geylang and Katong.

The ride Each air-conditioned capsule accommodates up to 28 people. There are two screens in each capsule but, disappointingly, these broadcast commercials and funk music rather than any commentary on the landmarks (though you will be informed when you've reached the top of the ride). There's also a three-story airport terminal-style building at the base of the wheel, featuring shopping and dining options.

More to See

ARAB STREET

Good handicrafts from all over Asia can be bought near the intersection of Beach Road and Arab Street, where some of the area's original shops still survive. Look for basketware, textiles, lace, silverwork, jewelry and perfume. This is the best part of Singapore for buying fabric; numerous shops offer silks, cottons and batiks, and there are plenty of relaxed eateries in the area too.

G4/5 Between North Bridge Road and Beach Road Bugis

BUGIS STREET

Bugis Street was rebuilt in 1991, 449ft (137m) from its original site. It's two sections, either side of Victoria Street, contrast sharply. The western stretch is most fun and contains the largest covered outdoor market in town (as well as possibly the largest ceiling fan on earth). There are clothes, crafts and curios as well as a selection of snacks and drinks. There are heaps of fruit and veg stalls near Albert Street. Bugis Street east of Victoria Street is dominated by the Bugis Junction shopping plaza, a collection of brand name shops and indie stores in air-conditioned surrounds that still manage to preserve the old shophouse facades.

F5 Bugis Street Outdoor market open daily until midnight. Bars open daily to 2 or 3am Fast-food outlets Bugis 2, 5, 7, 12, 32, 61, 62, 63, 84, 130, 160, 197, 520, 851, 960 Few (pedestrian precinct) Moderate bars and food, antiques and crafts

CHETTIAR'S TEMPLE

www.sttemple.com

The temple of Sri Thandayuthanapani, rebuilt in 1984, is also called Chettiar's Temple after the Indian *chettiars* (moneylenders) who financed its construction in the 1850s. The *gopuram* is a riot of images and colors. Each glass panel of the unusual 48-panel ceiling frieze, from India, features a deity from the Hindu pantheon.

E6 15 Tank Road 6737 9393 Daily 8–12, 5.30–8.30 Dhoby Ghaut Free

Outside Chettiar's Temple

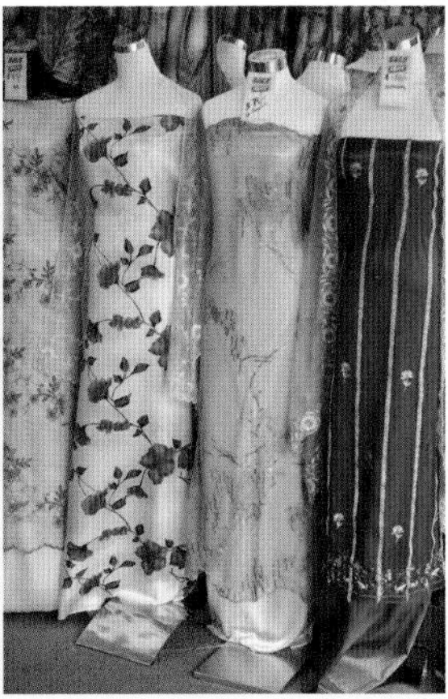

Arab Street shop display

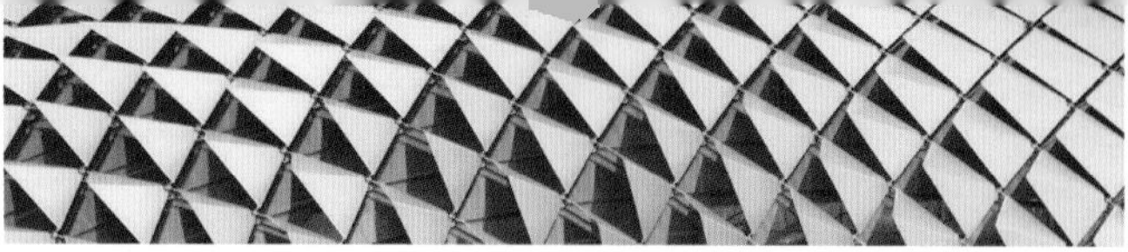

ESPLANADE—THEATRES ON THE BAY

www.esplanade.com

A stunning waterfront theater and entertainment complex, dubbed the Durians for its two prickly domes, hosts a wide array of local and international performers in world-class facilities that include the Concert Hall (1,600 seats), Lyric Theatre (2,000 seats) and an outdoor stage that often offers free performances.

F6 1 Esplanade Drive 6828 8377 Daily 10–10; 45-min tours Tue–Fri at 9, 12.30, 2, Sat–Sun at 9 Esplanade Good Tours moderate

MINT MUSEUM OF TOYS

www.emint.com

This five-floor museum brings in toys from 25 countries, including some rare and valuable antiques up to a century old. The exhibitions will likely induce nostalgia among big kids and high excitement among adult collectors, though there's educational value for younger visitors with some hands-on displays. Mr Punch restaurant (in the basement) and Winebar (on the roof) are both worth a visit. There are also collectables on hand, thematically linked to the toys in the main exhibition.

F5 26 Seah Street 6339 0660 Daily 9.30–6.30 Restaurant and bar City Hall, Bugis Good Moderate

MUSEUM OF SHANGHAI TOYS

www.shanghaitoys.wordpress.com

The world's first museum to exclusively show toys originating from China, the compact museum has three levels of exhibition space. Look out for such delightful and nostalgic exhibits as an electric tram from the 1920s, an Ada Lunn Doll dating from the1950s, and an ethnic doll from the1960s. There is a souvenir and retail shop on the ground floor.

F4 83 Rowell Road 6294 7747 Tue–Sat 11–7, Sun 11–6 Farrer Park Good Moderate

THE PADANG

Once the Padang directly faced the sea, but land reclamation in

Mickey Mouse exhibit at the Mint Museum of Toys

Padang baseball player

Marina Bay has long since changed its outlook. This huge rectangular lawn—*padang* means "field" in Malay— which goes back to Raffles' days, has retained its use as a recreational area. Cricket and rugby matches are played in season and while nonmembers may not venture into the clubs, they can stand and watch the games. City Hall, facing the Padang, has seen several historic events: the herding of Europeans onto the Padang on the morning of the Japanese occupation, and the formal surrender of the Japanese on its steps in 1945. At the southern end is the Cricket Club, the hub of colonial society in the 19th century, with a commanding view of the Padang. The group of government buildings includes the attorney-general's chambers (resembling a small opera house), the Victoria Theatre and Concert Hall buildings, and the former Parliament House.

F6 3 St Andrew's Road City Hall 10, 70, 75, 82, 97, 100, 107, 125, 130, 131, 167, 196 None Free

PERANAKAN MUSEUM

www.peranakanmuseum.org.sg

This excellent museum is on the site of the original Asian Civilisations Museum at the edge of Fort Canning Park. It documents Singapore's most fascinating minority race, the Peranakans. This slightly ambiguous term refers to descendents of mixed-race marriages between Malays and Chinese or Indian settlers. The displays focus mainly on the Chinese Peranakan culture. The first floor is given over to Peranakan wedding rituals, with more focused exhibits on fashion, eating and religion on the second floor—and both give a fascinating insight into how the Peranakans, and Singaporeans, have learned to blend cultures. To better understand the meaning of "Peranakan," begin your visit by watching the talking heads video on the second floor.

E5/6 39 Armenian Street 6332 7591 Mon 1–6, Tue–Sun 9–7 (until 9pm Fri) Restaurants and cafés nearby Bras Basah Good Inexpensive. Free Fri 7–9

Wedding chamber in the Peranakan Museum

RED DOT MUSEUM

www.museum.red-dot.sg

Housed within a striking scarlet-washed colonial building that once played home to the Singaporean traffic police, the red dot design museum is a fascinating exhibition space that showcases award winners from Germany's highly respected red dot organization. The displays are divided between imaginative design concepts yet to be given commercial backing, and finished products that have set the standard in their field, spanning everything from mechanized gadgetry to children's toys. Despite the size of the building, this is not a huge space, divided between one large industrial room and a spotlighted gallery, but is one of only two of its kind in the world. The first weekend of the month the museum is host to MAAD market, when local artists and designers set up stalls to sell their stuff.

E8 GF, Red Dot Traffic Building, 28 Maxwell Road 6327 8027 Mon–Tue, Fri, 11–6, Sat–Sun 11–8 Maxwell Road Food Centre nearby Tanjong Pagar Good Moderate Occasionally closed for private events so call ahead

SRI MARIAMMAN TEMPLE

This is Singapore's oldest Hindu temple, a Technicolor shrine with brilliant statuary on the tower. It is dedicated to the goddess Mariamman, said to have powers to cure epidemics such as cholera and smallpox. The temple shows the three principal elements of Dravidian architecture: an interior shrine (*vimanam*) covered by a decorated dome, an assembly hall (*madapam*) used for prayers and an entrance tower (*gopuram*) covered with painted Hindu deities. The preferred venue for most Hindu weddings, the temple is still very much a place of worship; respect this and remember to remove your footwear before entering.

E7 244 South Bridge Road 6223 4064 Daily 7–12, 6–9.30 Chinatown SBS bus 103, 166, 167 from City Hall None Free

The red dot museum

Statue in the Sri Mariamman Temple

Around Singapore's Historic Core

Get a feel for both the old and new Singapore with this long walk that includes temples and the grand Raffles Hotel.

DISTANCE: 5 miles (8km) **ALLOW:** 5 hours

START

MAXWELL ROAD
E7 Tanjong Pagar

❶ From Maxwell Road walk down South Bridge Road to visit the Buddha Tooth Relic Temple (▷ 26). Turn left down South Street and return to South Bridge Road via Trengganu and Pagoda streets.

❷ Note the renovated Chinese shophouses and visit the Sri Mariamman Temple (▷ 44). Cross over and take Ann Siang Hill, then turn left down Club Street.

❸ Turn right at Cross Street and left into Telok Ayer Street. Far East Square and China Square are full of places to eat. Check out Fuk Tak Chi Museum.

❹ Turn right down Cheang Hong Lim Place and left at the end of Church Street and follow Market Street and Malacca Place in Raffles Place. Head north to reach Bonham Street and turn left into Boat Quay.

❺ Walk along the riverbank until you come to Cavenagh Bridge.

❻ Cross and pass Empress Place on the riverside promenade before turning right into Old Parliament Lane to pass the Victoria Concert Hall and Theatre. On the right is Singapore Cricket Club. Cross over High Street and take St Andrew's Road. The Padang is on your right.

❼ After Raffles City is Raffles Hotel (▷ 38). Continue along Beach Road. Turn left onto Arab Street, right onto Baghdad Street and left onto Bussorah Street. Facing Sultan Mosque, take the side street to your left, then head up Arab Street to Victoria Street.

❽ Wander around the streets lined with old shops selling cloth and handicrafts. Return to your hotel.

END

ARAB STREET
G4 Bugis

Shopping

313@SOMERSET
www.313somerset.com.sg
Set up above the Somerset MRT station, this eight-floor mall offers an eclectic mix of fashion brands. Home to everything from Forever 21's Singapore flagship to a range of shops from contemporary European designers.
D5 313 Orchard Road 6496 9313 Sun–Thu 10–10. Fri–Sat 10am–11pm Somerset

CENTREPOINT
www.fraserscentrepointmalls.com
One of the most user-friendly complexes, with good department stores (Robinson's and Marks & Spencer) and shops selling everything from books to clothes and electrical goods, plus restaurants and a supermarket.
D5 176 Orchard Road 6737 9000 Daily 10–10 Somerset

CHINATOWN POINT
One of Chinatown's earliest shopping centers, containing a variety of shops and eateries, and specializing in local handicraft and gift shops.
E7 133 New Bridge Road 6702 0114 Daily 10–10 Chinatown

FUNAN DIGITALIFE MALL
www.funan.com.sg
A huge range of computers and accessories, as well as photographic equipment.
F6 109 North Bridge Road 6336 8327 Daily 10–10 City Hall

THE HEEREN
www.heeren.com.sg
Popular among the hip and trendy. Browse vintage shops on the fourth and fifth floors or sip coffee at Spinelli's outdoor café.
D5 260 Orchard Road 6738 4388 Daily 10am–11pm Somerset

ION ORCHARD
www.ionorchard.com
Architecturally stunning on the outside, the choice of more than 300 shops inside this modern mall is equally awesome. Top brands like Louis Vuitton, Prada, Burberry and Dior can all be found within these futuristic walls.
C4 2 Orchard Turn 6238 8228 Daily 10–10 Orchard

HONG BAO
You may notice small red packets on sale. These *hong bao*, as they are known, are used for giving gifts of money, particularly for weddings and at Chinese New Year, when it is the custom for unmarried children to receive a red packet. Many employers also choose this time of year to give their red packets—bonuses.

LUCKY PLAZA
www.luckyplazashopping.com
Another huge shopping complex, full of small shops selling all manner of goods. Salespeople may be aggressive, so bargain hard.
D5 304 Orchard Road 6235 3294 Daily 10–7 (but individual shop times vary) Orchard

MANDARIN GALLERY
www.mandaringallery.com.sg
A sophisticated addition to the shopping strip, the gallery is home to quality labels such as Boss, Armani and Marc by Marc Jacobs, along with Singapore's top designer, Ashley Isham's, boutique.
D5 333 Orchard Road 6831 6363 Daily 11–9.30 Somerset

MATA HARI ANTIQUES
The basketry, lacquerware and silver jewelry here originate from Thailand, Cambodia, Vietnam, Indonesia and Burma.
E7 13 Ann Siang Hill 6737 6068 Wed–Sun 12–8 Chinatown

MILLENIA WALK
More than 190 designer and street-smart fashion stores and specialty shops, such as Raoul, jewelers like the Hour Glass and Cortina E'space, and electrical superstore Harvey Norman.
G6 9 Raffles Boulevard 6883 1122 Daily 10–10 City Hall

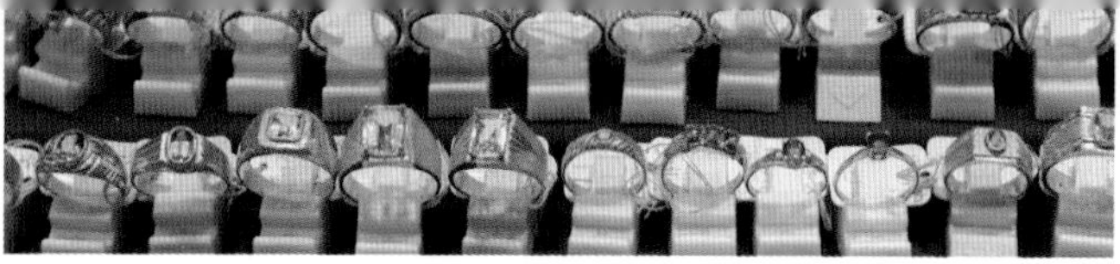

MUSTAFA CENTRE
www.mustafa.com.sg
More than 75,000 items over four floors in Singapore's only 24-hour mall. Clothing, CDs, jewelry and cameras are just some of the items you can pick up here. Great for bargain-hunters.
F3 145 Syed Alwi Road 6295 5855 24 hours, 7 days Farrer Park

ORCHARD CENTRAL
www.orchardcentral.com.sg
Filled with shops catering to the rising hipster community of Singapore, alternative fashion can be checked out in places like The Reckless Shop or Pact—a restaurant, hair salon and specially curated boutique all in one.
D5 181 Orchard Road 6238 1051 Daily 11–10 Somerset

PEOPLE'S PARK COMPLEX
You can buy all manner of goods at this bustling complex in the heart of Chinatown, including traditional remedies and Asian textiles. There are plenty of clothing and electronic shops, too. This is one of the city's oldest shopping centers.
E7 1 Park Road 6535 9533 Daily 10–9.45 Outram Park

RAFFLES CITY
www.rafflescity.com.sg
The four-story mall section of this IM Pei-designed "city within a city" has floors dedicated to luxury buyers, fashionistas and children. It's one of Singapore's most accessible malls, easily reached from the City Hall interchange.
G4 252 North Bridge Road 6338 7766 Daily 10–9.30 City Hall

SUNTEC CITY MALL
www.sunteccity.com.sg
Shoppers are welcomed by the Fountain of Wealth at one of Singapore's largest shopping malls. You'll find brand-name stores and specialty shops, including the G2000 flagship store and Mango.
G5 3 Temasek Boulevard 6825 2667 Daily 10–10 Esplanade or Promenade

TANGS
www.tangs.com
This popular department store has shelf after shelf of fashions and accessories.
C4 320 Orchard Road 6737 5500 Mon–Thu 10.30–9.30, Fri–Sat 10.30–11, Sun 11–8.30 Orchard

BARGAINING

Many Singapore shopkeepers are happy for you to bargain with them and it can save you a significant percentage, even on fairly small purchases. Don't make your first offer until the seller has reduced the opening price at least once. It is considered a matter of honor that once you have settled on a price, you must go through with the deal. Don't bargain if you see "Fixed price" signs.

TEMPLE/PAGODA/TRENGGANU STREETS
In the streets between South Bridge Road and New Bridge Road, in the heart of Chinatown, shops and stalls sell a tantalizing range of Chinese goods: herbal remedies, porcelain, exotic fruit and gold jewelry. The rich smell of barbecued pork pervades the streets.
E7 Off South Bridge Road Chinatown

THIEVES MARKET
The ultimate bargain haunt in Singapore, with down-at-heel vendors selling second-hand goods at the roadside. Bargaining is essential, and things only get into full swing after sundown.
F5 Sungei Road Daily 11–7 Bugis

YUE HWA CHINESE PRODUCTS EMPORIUM
www.yuehwa.com.sg
This well laid-out Chinatown department store has an array of quality merchandise, from traditional clothes to handicrafts, food and household items.
E7 70 Eu Tong Sen Street 6538 4222 Sun–Fri 11–9, Sat 11–10 Chinatown

Entertainment and Nightlife

1-ALTITUDE

www.1-altitude.com

The highest rooftop bar in Singapore, 1-Altitude occupies the top three floors in One Raffles Place: a sports bar on Level 61, European restaurant Stellar on 62 and alfresco bar with great views on 63.

F7 1 Raffles Place 6438 0410 Mon–Thu 6pm–2am, Fri–Sat 6pm–4am, Sun 6pm–1am Raffles Place

28 HONGKONG STREET

www.28hks.com

It's easy to wander past the entrance without noticing, as there is no signage outside. Some of the best and priciest cocktails in the city.

E6 28 Hong Kong Street 6533 2001 Mon–Thu 5.30pm–1am, Fri–Sat 5.30pm–3am Clarke Quay

BLU JAZ CAFÉ

www.blujaz.net

A friendly, laid-back jazz spot at the southern edge of Kampong Glam, just off Haji Lane. There's live music nightly after 9pm.

G5 11 Bali Lane, Kampong Glam 6292 3800 Bugis Mon–Thu noon–1am, Fri noon–2am, Sat 4pm–2am

CLUB KYO

www.clubkyo.com

Set up in the heart of the CBD, Kyo gives off a hip underground vibe. Attracting a range of local DJs, this 6,000sq ft space can accommodate up to 220. The bar is rumored to be the longest in Singapore. The dress code does not allow flip-flops or sandals and an entry charge applies after 10pm on Saturdays and Sundays.

F7 133 Cecil Street 8299 8735 Wed–Thu 9pm–3am, Fri–Sat 9pm–late Tanjong Pagar

CRAZY ELEPHANT

www.crazyelephant.com

One of the oldest venues in Clarke Quay, the walls in Singapore's premier rock 'n' roll blues bar are covered with graffiti from past patrons.

E6 01-03 Clarke Quay, 3E River Valley Road 6337 7859 Sun–Thu 5pm–2am, Fri–Sat 5pm–3am Clarke Quay

WHAT'S ON

Concerts and theater are very popular, particularly for weekend shows. Details of events, their venues and where to buy tickets can be found in Singapore's daily morning newspaper, the *Straits Times,* and various free publications. Tickets are obtainable from SISTIC and TicketCharge outlets at Centrepoint, Tanglin Mall, Wisma Atria, Great World City, Raffles City Shopping Centre, Takashimaya Store, Funan Centre, Junction 8 and Bugis Junction. Bookings 6348 5555 and 6296 2929.

THE CUFFLINK CLUB

www.thecufflinkclub.com

The bartenders at this swanky cocktail lounge focus on shaking up the perfect tipple. Often filled with after-work executives looking for a bit of downtime.

E7 6 Jiak Chuan Road 9694 9623 Mon–Thu 5pm–1am, Fri 5pm–2am, Sat 6pm–2am Outram Park

THE DUBLINER IRISH PUB

www.dublinersingapore.com

Set in a former colonial mansion, this popular pub, with its plush interior, serves excellent food.

E5 165 Penang Road 6735 2220 Daily noon–2am Dhoby Ghaut

HARRY'S @ BOAT QUAY

A riverside location makes this one of Singapore's most popular places for a drink, and the crowd often spills out onto the sidewalk. Blues on Sunday, jazz Wednesday to Saturday.

E6 28 Boat Quay 6538 3029 Mon–Thu 11am–midnight, Fri, Sat 11am–3am, Sun 11am–1am 16, 31, 55

KU DÉ TA

www.kudeta.com.sg

The bar/restaurant perched on top of Marina Bay Sands is modeled

after one of the most popular hang-outs in Bali. There are great views of the city, and entrance is free before 9pm.
G7 1 Bayfront Avenue 6688 7688 Daily 11am–late Bayfront

LONG BAR AND BAR & BILLARDS ROOM

The Singapore Sling is usually high on a visitor's list of things to taste in Singapore, and the place to enjoy it is undoubtedly the Bar and Billiards Room and the Long Bar, both in the Raffles Hotel (▷ 38), where the drink was first served.
F5 Raffles Hotel Arcade 6337 1886 Sun–Thu 11am–1am, Fri, Sat 6pm–2am City Hall

LOOF

www.loof.com.sg
This rooftop bar is an eccentric, artsy affair and majors in down tempo electronica. One for budding artists, designers and fashionistas.
G4 03-07 Odean Towers, 331 North Bridge Road 9773 9304 Mon–Thu 5pm–1am, Fri–Sat 5pm–3am City Hall

NEW ASIA BAR

The New Asia Bar boasts great views. It's best for a drink at dusk.
F6 72F, The Swissotel, 2 Stamford Road 9177 7307 Sun–Tue 5pm–1am, Wed–Thu 5pm–2am, Fri–Sat 5pm–3am City Hall Dress code after 9pm

PALONG LOBBY BAR

Located in the Rendezvous Hotel, you get great cocktails in tranquil surroundings.
E5 9 Bras Basah Road 6335 1880 Daily noon–11 Dhoby Ghaut

PAULANER BRAHAUS

Serves Authentic Bavarian cuisine and popular Munich beer in a range of types. The rustic setting is reminiscent of German microbreweries.
F6 01-01 Millenia Walk, 9 Raffles Boulevard 6883 2572 Sun–Thu 11.30am–1am, Fri, Sat 11.30am–2am 32, 54, 195 City Hall

ONE FOR THE ROAD

After working a 10- to 12-hour day, your average Singaporean either heads home to relax with family members, or, if they are young and single, stops at a favorite bar for a drink en route. Weekends see increased nightlife activity; clubs do a roaring trade and attract expats and locals alike, especially those in the courting mode. As in other large cities, there is a good selection of Irish pubs and October brings a quota of German-inspired beer fests. And don't leave the city without having a Singapore Sling at the famous Long Bar at Raffles Hotel (▷ 38).

POST BAR

Part of the stylish Fullerton hotel (▷ 112), this bar serves classic and fruity cocktails.
F6 1 Fullerton Square 6877 8135 Mon–Fri noon–2am, Sat, Sun 5pm–2am Raffles Place

THE PUMP ROOM

www.pumproomasia.com
A combined microbrewery, bistro and bar, Pump Room is one of Clarke Quay's hotspots come night time. A live band plays pop, rock and jazz.
E6 Clarke Quay, 3B River Valley Road 6334 2628 Sun–Fri 5pm–3am, Sat 5pm–4am Clarke Quay

LA TERRAZA ROOFTOP BAR

www.screeningroom.com.sg
The rooftop bar at Screening Room, an entertainment venue that offers movie screenings paired with the perfect meal, is a unique spot to spend the evening.
E7 12 Ann Siang Road 6221 1694 Mon–Thu 6pm–1am, Fri–Sat 6pm–3am Chinatown

ZOUK

www.zoukclub.com
Five different clubs make up Singapore's longest-running nightlife venue. Excellent in-house and guest DJs spin the latest hot dance music tracks.
D6 17-21 Jiak Kim Street 6738 2988 Times vary, but all venues stay open late 16, 75, 175

Restaurants

PRICES

Prices are approximate, based on a 3-course meal for one person.
$$$ over S$50
$$ S$20–S$50
$ under S$20

BENG THIN HOON KEE ($)

Hokkien food is popular in Singapore, for the ancestors of many Singaporeans lived in southern China, where the cuisine originated. Try duck in lotus leaves.
F7 05–02 OCBC Building, 65 Chulia Street 6533 7708 Daily 11.30–3, 6–10 Raffles Place

BLUE GINGER ($$)

www.theblueginger.com
Set in an old shophouse, this is the best place in Singapore to try Peranakan dishes such as fried pork and prawn rolls, *ayam panggang* (chicken in coconut milk) and durian desserts.
E8 97 Tanjong Pagar Road, Chinatown 6222 3928 Daily 12–2.30, 6.30–10.30 Tanjong Pagar

CATALUNYA ($$$)

www.catalunya.sg
This contemporary Spanish restaurant is in a glass-enclosed dome overlooking Marina Bay. Creative tapas are whipped up by award-winning chefs.
F7 The Fullerton Pavilion, 82 Collyer Quay 6534 0188 Daily noon–2am Raffles Place

CHINA SQUARE ($)

This sprawling three-floor food complex has Western food outlets and traditional hawker fare under one roof.
E7 51 Telok Ayer Street Daily 7am–10pm Tanjong Pagar

CHINATOWN FOOD STREET ($)

Following a S$4 million dollar revamp, this side street is still lined with open-air stalls that come into their own after dark. Most types of local Chinese food are available plus a range of desserts—try the ice *kacang*.
E7 Smith Street Early until late, daily Chinatown

SATAY

No trip to Singapore would be complete without the famous satay, a Malay dish. Sticks of chicken, lamb or beef, and sometimes other foods such as tofu, are barbecued and served with a thick, sweet peanut sauce. Small rice cakes and cucumber usually accompany the satay. It is served in some restaurants, and at many hawker centers. You can buy ready-made satay sauce to try at home with a barbecue.

CRYSTAL JADE ($$)

www.crystaljade.com
Traditional Cantonese cuisine including fresh seafood, barbecued pork and soups. This Asia-wide chain also serves arguably the best dim sum in town.
C4 04-20 Ngee Ann City, 391 Orchard Road 6238 1661 Daily 11.30–2.30, 6.30–10.30 Orchard

INDOCHINE ($$$)

www.indochine-group..com
The original haunt of what is now a global brand is tucked away in Chinatown. Vietnamese/Cambodian/Laotian dishes include spicy sausage and fried fish. There are four other branches in Singapore, including the lavish Forbidden City at Clarke Quay.
E7 47 Club Street 6323 0503 Mon–Fri 12–10.30, Sat 6–10.30pm Chinatown

KOMALA VILAS ($)

Vegetarian Indian fare is served here on banana leaves. It's good and inexpensive, and you can have unlimited helpings. Try the sweet, spicy *masala* tea.
F4 76–78 Serangoon Road 6293 6980 Daily 7am–10.30pm Little India

LOLLA ($$$)

www.lolla.com.sg
Listed as one of Zagat's "10 hottest restaurants in

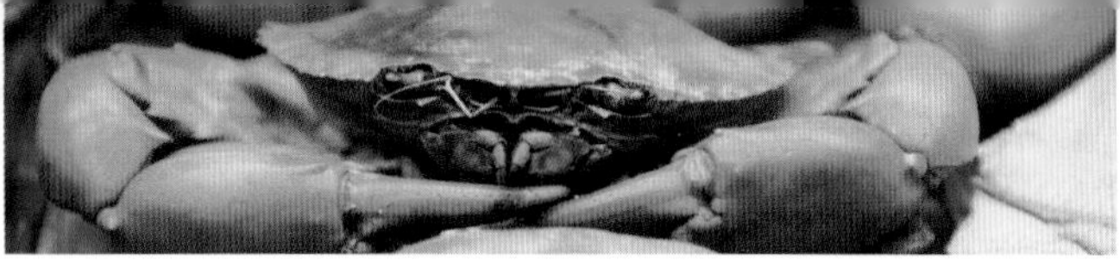

the world" in 2013, this Mediterranean-influenced tapas bar was developed from an underground supper club. Grab a counter seat at the ground floor's open kitchen to watch the chefs.
E7 22 Ann Siang Road 6423 1228 Daily noon–2, 6–midnight Chinatown

PASTA BRAVA ($$)
www.pastabrava.com.sg
A lovely Italian restaurant in a converted shophouse on the edge of Chinatown. Some dishes can be expensive, but the food is very good. This place is popular with workers at lunch.
E8 11 Craig Road 6227 7550 Mon–Sat 11.30–2.30, 6.30–10.30 Tanjong Pagar

PAULANER BRÄUHAUS ($$)
www.paulaner.com.sg
German theme restaurant-cum-brewery serving generous platters of *sauerkraut* and *wurst kartoffeln*.
F6 01-01 Millenia Walk, 9 Raffles Boulevard 6883 2572 Daily 12–2.30, 6.30–10.30 (drinks only after 10) Promenade

PETE'S PLACE ($$$)
This basement trattoria is popular with both visitors and locals. The pastas are tasty and an excellent salad bar makes it a good bet for vegetarians.
C4 Basement, Grand Hyatt Hotel, 10–12 Scotts Road 6730 7113 Daily 12–3, 6–11, Sun brunch 11.30–2.30 Orchard

PREGO ($$$)
This long-established restaurant bustles at lunch and in the evenings thanks to excellent dishes and a central location.
F6 Swissotel The Stamford, 2 Stamford Road 6431 5156 Daily 11.30–2.30, 6.30–10.30 City Hall

RANG MAHAL ($$$)
This restaurant has moved to the ultramodern Pan Pacific Hotel but is still serving a good range of North Indian dishes and an extensive lunch and dinner buffet.
G6 Level 3, Pan Pacific Hotel, Raffles Boulevard 6333 1788 Daily 12–2.30, 6.30–10.30 City Hall

RESTAURANT EMBER
This small and hip restaurant is part of the boutique backpackers joint, Hotel 1929. Singaporean chef Sebastian Ng serves up both straight-laced European dishes and racy fusion concoctions.
E6 Ground floor, Hotel 1929, 50 Keong Saik Road 6347 1928 Mon–Fri 11.30–2, 6.30–10, Sat 6.30–10 Outram Park

POPIAH

Popiah—freshly prepared rice-flour pancakes filled with a mouthwatering mixture of onion, turnip, bean sprouts, minced pork and prawns, all held together with a sweet soy sauce and flavored with coriander, garlic and chili—make a delicious snack. Many hawker centers have a *popiah* stall.

SRI VIJAYA ($)
Modest vegetarian, banana-leaf establishment offering great value with its generous helpings of rice and vegetable accompaniments.
F4 229 Selegie Road 6336 1748 Daily 9–9 Little India

SUPERNATURE ($)
www.supernature.com.sg
Soy burgers, healthy sandwiches and fresh juices are the staples at this chic organic shop. Vegans are well catered to.
C5 B1-05 Forum, 583 Orchard Road 6735 4338 Mon–Sat 10–7, Sun 11–6 Orchard

YUM CHA ($$)
www.yumcha.com.sg
Visit on the weekends and select delicious dim sum from push carts. Framed photos of Chinatown in the 1960s give you an idea of what the area was like back in the day.
E7 20 Trengganu Street (off Temple Street), 02-01 6372 1717 Mon–Fri 11–11, Sat–Sun 9am–11pm Chinatown

West Island

Head west for the world's best bird park, a patch of original tropical rainforest, and hedonistic Sentosa, the recreational hub of this dynamic island nation.

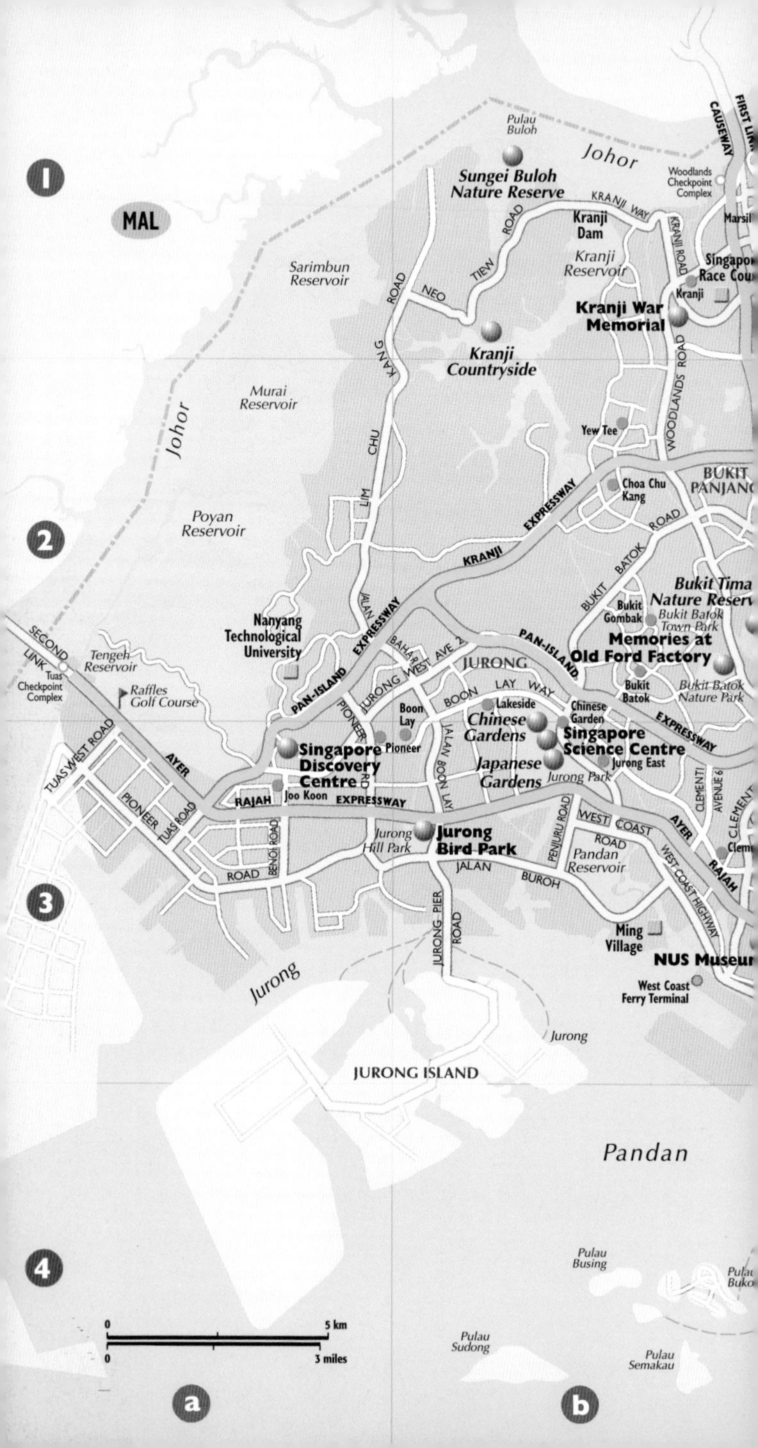

MAL
Johor
Pulau Buloh
Sungei Buloh Nature Reserve
Kranji Dam
Kranji Reservoir
Kranji War Memorial
Kranji Countryside
Woodlands Checkpoint Complex
CAUSEWAY
Singapore Race Course
Kranji
KRANJI WAY
KRANJI ROAD
TIEW ROAD
NEO
LIM CHU KANG ROAD
WOODLANDS ROAD
Sarimbun Reservoir
Murai Reservoir
Poyan Reservoir
Yew Tee
Choa Chu Kang
BUKIT PANJANG
KRANJI EXPRESSWAY
BUKIT BATOK ROAD
Bukit Timah Nature Reserve
Bukit Gombak
Bukit Batok Town Park
Memories at Old Ford Factory
Bukit Batok
Bukit Batok Nature Park
Nanyang Technological University
JALAN BAHAR
PAN-ISLAND EXPRESSWAY
JURONG WEST AVE 2
JURONG
BOON LAY WAY
SECOND LINK
Tuas Checkpoint Complex
Tengeh Reservoir
Raffles Golf Course
Lakeside
Chinese Gardens
Chinese Garden
Singapore Science Centre
Japanese Gardens
Jurong Park
Jurong East
Boon Lay
Pioneer
PIONEER RD
JALAN BOON LAY
Singapore Discovery Centre
Joo Koon
AYER RAJAH EXPRESSWAY
TUAS WEST ROAD
PIONEER ROAD
TUAS ROAD
BENOI ROAD
Jurong Hill Park
Jurong Bird Park
JALAN BUROH
PENJURU ROAD
WEST COAST ROAD
Pandan Reservoir
WEST COAST HIGHWAY
CLEMENTI AVENUE 6
Ming Village
NUS Museum
West Coast Ferry Terminal
JURONG PIER ROAD
Jurong
JURONG ISLAND
Pandan
Pulau Busing
Pulau Sudong
Pulau Semakau
0
5 km
3 miles
1
2
3
4
a
b

MAL
SEMBAWANG
Sembawan Beach
ADMIRALTY ROAD
WOODLANDS AVENUE 7
CANBERRA LINK
Sembawang
Admiralty
Woodlands
WOODLANDS
WOODLANDS AVENUE 12
Pulau Seletar
Johor
Pulau Punggol Barat
Pulau Punggol Timor
Yishun
YISHUN
ROAD
SEMBAWANG
Yishun Park
Khatib
SELETAR
EXPRESSWAY
MANDAI ROAD
MANDAI AVE
Lower Seletar Reservoir
Singapore Zoo and River Safari
Night Safari
Upper Seletar Reservoir
Central Catchment Nature Reserve
UPPER THOMPSON ROAD
Upper Peirce Reservoir
MacRitchie Trail
MacRitchie Reservoir
PAN-ISLAND EXPRESSWAY
LORNIE ROAD
TOA PAYOH
DUNEARN ROAD
BUKIT TIMAH ROAD
Botanic Gardens
HOLLAND ROAD
Farrer Road
Colonial Residences
Holland Village
COMMONWEALTH AVENUE
ORCHARD ROAD
Buona Vista
Commonwealth
NAPIER RD
DEMPSEY HILL
One-North
EXPRESSWAY
Queenstown
ALEXANDRA ROAD
Redhill
JALAN BUKIT MERAH
Tiong Bahru
Kent Ridge
Haw Par Villa
Telok Blangah Hill Park
COAST HIGHWAY
115
Mount Faber
Pasir Panjang
Labrador Park
Telok Blangah
HarbourFront
HarbourFront
GATEWAY AVENUE
Pulau Brani
Sentosa
Pulau Tekukor
Pulau Seringat
Pulau Jong
Pulau Sakijang Bendera
St John's Island
Pulau Tembakul
Kusu Island
Pulau Sebarok
Pulau Darat
Pulau Subar Laut
Pulau Sakijang Pelepah
Lazarus
c
d

Botanic Gardens

TOP 25

HIGHLIGHTS

- Rubber trees
- National Orchid Garden
- Jungle Walk
- Palm Valley
- *Myristica fragans* (nutmeg tree)
- *Cinnamomum zeylanicum* (cinnamon tree)
- Topiary
- Bamboos
- Herbarium

TIP

- Go to www.sbg.org.sg for details of the free concerts that are held on the Show Foundation Symphony Stage.

Don't leave Singapore without a visit to this botanical wonder, with its splendid National Orchid Garden. It is best explored in the relative cool of the morning or the evening.

Botanical beginnings Singapore's tranquil botanic gardens are only a few miles from frenetic Orchard Road. Sir Stamford Raffles established botanical gardens at the base of Government Hill in 1822, and the collection was moved to its present site in 1859. Over the decades, the gardens have been enlarged and landscaped. The region's first rubber trees, native to Brazil, were propagated here in 1877, and their descendants remain in the gardens. In the 1960s, the gardens supplied many of the seedlings for roadsides and parks all over the island, and the greening of Singapore began.

Clockwise from left: the National Orchid Garden; close-up from the National Orchid Garden; the Ginger Garden; the National Orchid Garden; the entrance gate and the Evolution Garden

Highlights The National Orchid Garden has the largest display of tropical orchids in the world—more than 1,000 species and 2,000 hybrids—with a Cool House for high-altitude orchids and gardens with orchids in natural settings. On the rolling lawn of Palm Valley you'll find "islands" of various palms—more than 115 genera of the major plant group. The nearby patch of tropical rainforest is one of the few remaining areas of Singapore's original vegetation. Australian Black swans and many other water birds live around the Eco-Lake, where there are displays of herbs and spices, medicinal plants, fruit and nut trees, and bamboos. The visitor center has plant displays, water cascades, a café and a great selection of nature books in its excellent shop. The gardens are popular with locals, who jog, picnic and attend the frequent open-air concerts in Palm Valley.

THE BASICS

www.sbg.org.sg
c3, A4
1 Cluny Road
6471 7361
Daily 5am–midnight; National Orchid Garden daily 8.30am–7pm
Cafés and restaurants
Botanic Gardens
7, 75, 105, 106, 123, 174
Good
Botanic Gardens free; Orchid Garden inexpensive

Jurong Bird Park

TOP 25

HIGHLIGHTS

- Penguin feeding time
- Jungle Jewels
- Pelican Cove
- Waterfall Aviary
- World of Darkness
- Crowned pigeons
- Birds of paradise
- Southeast Asian hornbills and South American toucans

TIP

- The Breeding and Research Centre offers a behind-the-scenes look at how abandoned eggs and chicks are looked after.

Hundreds of penguins and puffins crowded together on an icy beach is an unexpected sight near the equator. And don't miss the Waterfall Aviary, where tropical bird species fly almost free.

The world's birds Jurong Bird Park is Asia-Pacific's biggest bird park—49 acres (20 hectares)—and home to more than 5,000 birds, many from the tropics. Some 380 species, from all over the world, are housed in aviaries and other apparently open enclosures.

Birds of a feather Not far from the entrance, penguins live in a simulated Antarctic habitat with a swimming area. The vast glass-sided tank has windows 98ft (30m) long. The Waterfall Aviary is the most spectacular area, with 5 acres (2 hec-

Clockwise from left: inside the Lory Loft; flamingoes in the water; the Birds 'n' Buddies show; feeding time; a parrot and waterfall in the park

tares) of forest contained beneath high netting, with more than 1,500 African birds. The aviary also has a 100ft (30m) man-made waterfall. Hop on board guided trams for a good overview of the park, or wander on foot to see birds close up. The Southeast Asian Birds Aviary is good for spotting local species; it re-creates a rainforest, even laying on a simulated storm at midday, and contains more than 260 species, including the colorful parrots. The African Wetlands exhibit, complete with native-style pavilions, includes the shoebill and African crowned crane. Jungle Jewels is a large walk-through aviary devoted to hummingbirds and other South American species. The birds of prey and parrot shows are also entertaining. Twice a day the Birds 'n' Buddies show features comedy, audience interaction and entertaining antics from the park's birds.

THE BASICS

www.birdpark.com.sg
b3, arrowed off at A7
2 Jurong Hill
6265 0022
Daily 8.30–6
Bongo Burgers, Hawk Café, Ben & Jerry's
MRT to Boon Lay then SBS bus 194 or 251
Good
Moderate
Bird shows: Kings of the Skies (10, 4), Birds 'n' Buddies (11, 3), Lunch with Parrots (1)

Night Safari

TOP 25

HIGHLIGHTS

- "Open" enclosures
- Leopard Trail
- Mouse deer
- Tapirs
- Giraffes
- Lions
- Tigers
- Hippos
- Elephants
- Bats
- Walking trails

TIP

- Check the weather forecast before venturing here, since rain spoils the whole experience somewhat.

Singapore's Night Safari—a zoo that allows you to see nocturnal animals—is the largest attraction of its kind in the world. Special lights that simulate moonlight illuminate this night zoo.

A world of animals The night safari is divided into eight "geographical" zones that are home to the park's 135 species—more than 2,000 animals in all. You can expect to see animals from the Southeast Asian rain forests, the African savanna, the Nepalese river valley, the South American pampas and the jungles of Myanmar (Burma). As in the Singapore Zoo, the enclosures are "open" and animals are confined by hidden walls and ditches. Five of these zones have dedicated walking tracks; the others must be visited by tram.

Clockwise from left: close up with the tapirs; the tram is the best way to see the animals; a baby anteater and Chawang, the Asian elephant

Welcome to the jungle The best way to see the Night Safari is to take the tram journey—the tram is silent to avoid frightening the animals. A guide offers commentary as you pass through. Get off at the tram stations and follow the marked walking trails through each zone. You can rejoin the tram anytime; all follow the same route. Avoid using a flash on your camera as it disturbs the animals and fellow visitors.

What to see Listen for the intermittent roaring of the big cats. The Leopard Trail is one of the busiest walking trails. You can see straight into the enclosure of the prowling leopards—only a plate-glass wall separates you from them. The Wallaby Trail is a more recent addition, inspired by the Australian Outback, and includes a cave filled with scorpions and venomous centipedes.

THE BASICS

www.nightsafari.com.sg
c2
80 Mandai Lake Road
6269 3411
Daily 7.30pm–midnight
Ulu Ulu Restaurant and gourmet Safari Express
Ang Mo Kio, then bus 138 or Choa Chu Kang, then bus 927
Reasonable
Expensive

Sentosa

TOP 25

HIGHLIGHTS

- Underwater World
- Images of Singapore
- Cable car
- Resorts World
- Tanjong Beach Club
- Sentosa Cove

TIP

- Weekends are busy and atmospheric but to avoid the crowds, visit midweek.

For long Singapore's playground, Sentosa has received several major facelifts over the past few years and is now home to world-class restaurants, rollercoasters spas and resorts.

Fun park Sentosa self-consciously caters to a variety of tastes, so if you're seeking the real Singapore, the island is probably not for you. Land reclamation and massive construction have turned this one-time pirates' lair into the closest thing Singapore has to Disneyland. It's still got a lovely green canopy covering, and there are quiet pockets, but Sentosa has become mass-market tourist heaven, with Universal Studios et al.

Rides and thrills In the past few years the island has filled with even more entertainment. In addi-

Clockwise from left: a resident of Sentosa Butterfly Park; golden statue on Sentosa; Underwater World; Siloso Beach and Southeast Asia (SEA) Aquarium of the Marine Life Park in Resort World

tion to the already popular Underwater World, which allows you to walk "through" the fish tanks in glass tunnels, part of the island is now home to the giant hotel and entertainment hub of Resorts World, which has an oceanarium, water park, Universal Studios, casino and six hotels. Over on Siloso Beach, adventure-seekers can try out iFly, an indoor skydiving wind tunnel, or the nearby Wave House for a simulated surf experience.

Child-free activities Along with all the restaurants that have popped up over the years, nightlife has developed on the island as well. Both Tanjong and Mambo beach clubs offer pool-side bars by the sea, with a variety of DJs visiting the decks regularly. Over at newly developed Sentosa Cove, W Hotel lures in many trendsetters and is also known to throw a good party.

THE BASICS

www.sentosa.com.sg
c4, arrowed off at B9
Just south of Singapore Island
Sentosa Information Centre 1800 736 8672
24 hours
Cafés and restaurants
Cable car from HarbourFront and Mount Faber
HarbourFront, then take Sentosa Express
Generally good
Individual venues may charge a cover

Singapore Discovery Centre

TOP 25

The Build It Kids Zone (left); the gateway (middle); the entrance (right) and Little George, the Centre's mascot (opposite)

THE BASICS

www.sdc.com.sg
- a3, arrowed off at A7
- 510 Upper Jurong Road
- 6792 6188
- Tue–Sun 9–6
- Restaurant and pizzeria
- Joo Koon
- Good
- Moderate

HIGHLIGHTS

- Visionarium
- Security Pavilion
- Interactive games
- iWERKS Theatre

The Discovery Centre is a world-class "edutainment" attraction that features Singapore's many milestones and achievements in five main galleries.

Visionarium The innovative high-tech exhibits, constructed around eight different themes, present a macro view of the Singapore Story and take you through Singapore's past, present and future, with brilliant light and sound shows and hands-on building activities. One of the highlights is the world's first and largest interactive team-based city design studio, the Visionarium, with a 360-degree screen. During each session, up to 120 guests can design a new city of Singapore and the result is displayed on the huge wraparound screen. A Security Pavilion, with a Crisis Simulation theater, simulates a bomb explosion at an MRT station.

Interactive games The Centre also has several entertaining interactive games and a lively quiz trivia show, located at the Unity Pavilion, and a simulated shooting range, where you can test your hand-eye coordination and shooting skills. Or you can try the even more challenging and exciting Crossfire Paintball. The On Location reporter will take you on a journey through Singapore's history and let you "report" on the nation's milestones.

iWERKS The iWERKS Theatre, next to the main exhibition hall, has a five-story-high screen and state-of-the-art sound system, and offers a truly unforgettable cinematic experience.

Singapore Nature Reserves

TOP 25

HIGHLIGHTS

Bukit Timah
- Macaques
- Strangler figs
- Bird hide
- Bike trail

MacRitchie Reservoir Park
- TreeTop Walk
- Birdlife
- Macaques

Sungei Buloh
- Mangrove walkways
- Estuarine crocodiles
- Free guided tours on Saturday

TIP

- The macaques can be a real nuisance here, so resist the temptation to feed them and watch that they don't snatch food from your hands.

Singapore is renowned for its green open spaces and, given its size, there are a surprising number of reserves where the original vegetation remains.

Bukit Timah The last remaining area of primary tropical rainforest in Singapore covers 410 acres (166 hectares) of Bukit Timah, Singapore's highest hill at 538ft (164m). Color-coded trails that start at the visitor area allow you to observe the reserve's fauna and flora, and a mountain bike trail is available for the more adventurous traveler.

MacRitchie Reservoir Park You can jog or walk on the shaded paths around the reservoir's edge; there are exercise stations at intervals. The highlight of several walks through the park, the 250yd/m TreeTop Walk, is along a freestanding

Bukit Timah Nature Reserve is home to Singapore's only remaining dipterocarps—emergent rainforest trees that can reach up to 230ft (70m) in height (left); Bukit Timah is rich in wildlife, from macaque monkeys down to lichens and bracket fungus (right)

suspension bridge that connects the park's two highest points. If it's not too busy, you can spot several animals along the way, including monitor lizards and fish eagles as well as long-tailed macaques, so don't have any food in sight.

Sungei Buloh Singapore's only wetland nature reserve covers 312 acres (130 hectares). Carefully planned walkways and strategically placed hides allow you to explore swamp, mangrove and mudflat habitats, and to observe tropical birdlife and many species of marine creatures, particularly mudskippers and crabs. Early morning and evening are the best times for viewing wildlife, with bird life most evident before 10am. From September to March, the reserve is home to migratory birds from as far afield as eastern Siberia.

THE BASICS

www.nparks.gov.sg
Bukit Timah
b2
177 Hindhede Drive
6468 5736
Daily 6am–7pm
MRT to Newton, then SBS bus 171 or TIBS 182, 65, 67, 75, 170, 171, 852, 961
None
Free

MacRitchie Reservoir Park
c2
Lornie Road
24 hours
Food kiosk
MRT to Newton, then bus 104, 132 or 167
Good
Free

Sungei Buloh
www.sbwr.org.sg
b1
301 Neo Tiew Crescent
6794 1401
7.30am–7pm Mon–Sat, 7–7 Sun and public hols
Take SMRT Bus 925 from Kranji MRT Station. Alight at Kranji Reservoir car park and walk for 15 min
Good
Mon–Fri free; Sat, Sun inexpensive

Singapore Science Centre

TOP 25

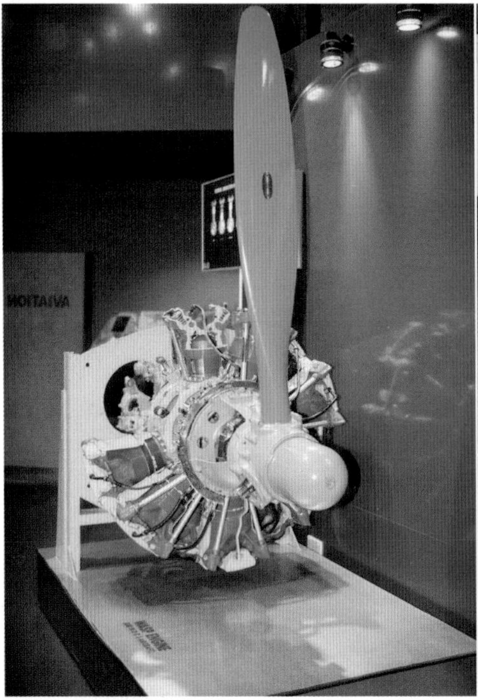
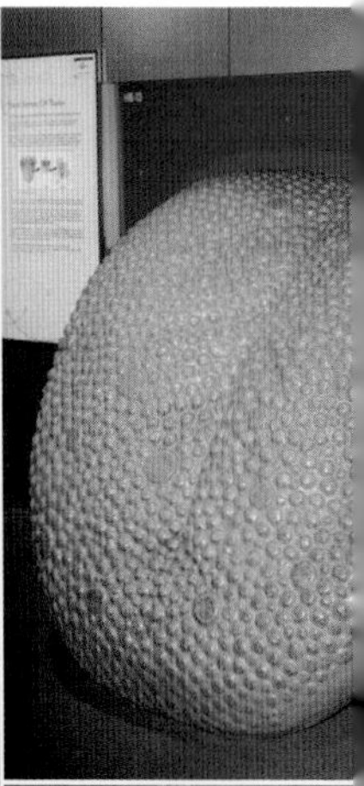

HIGHLIGHTS

- Atrium laser show
- Aviation Gallery
- Discovery Centre
- Ecogarden
- Omni-Theatre
- Waterworks

TIP

- The Science Centre shop has some excellent science kits and games for kids.

The world of science and wonder awaits at the Singapore Science Centre, which houses more than 1,000 exhibits. There are also hundreds of hands-on displays to excite children and enlighten adults.

Interactive exhibits The Singapore Science Centre attracts more than a million visitors each year. Theme galleries offer fascinating insights into human achievements in the physical and life sciences. Many of the exhibits are interactive, so this is a great place for families.

Science to hand The Waterworks Exhibition teaches about the importance of H_2O and also offers a cool-down on one of SIngapore's typically scorching days. The Climate Change show outlines in a humorous way the challenges we

Clockwise from left: Singapore Science Centre Aviation Gallery; a giant tongue at the Human Anatomy section; The World of Energy; the human anatomy section; the robotics section and the Atrium laser show

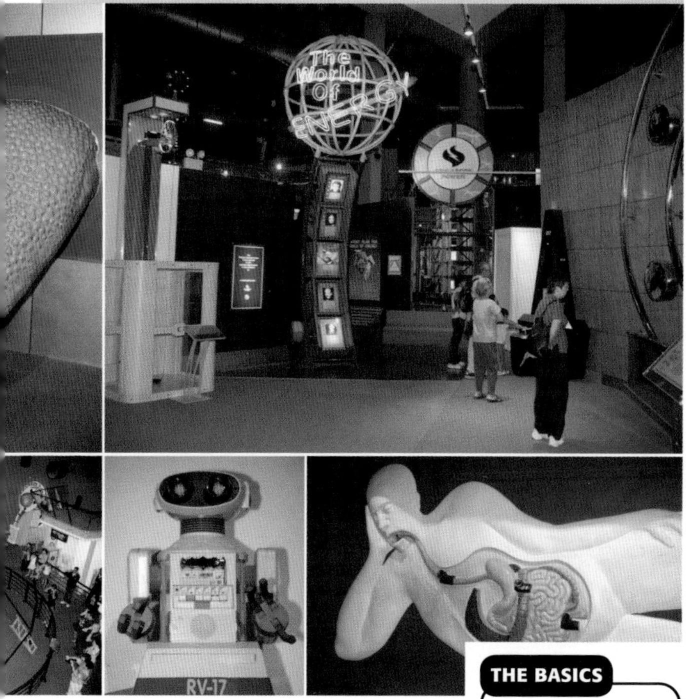

face in tackling global warming. Wander over to Uniquely You to explore genetics and the role it plays in each one of us. The Ecogarden is informative for horticulturalists, with its mini-orchard, hydroponic farm and medicinal garden.

Omni-Theatre and Observatory Next to the Science Centre is the Omni-Theatre. This theater was updated in 2014 with state-of-the-art projection and audio equipment with surround sound. You can see films on subjects as diverse as climbing Mt. Everest and the rule of China's first emperors. The features change every six months, so check to find out what's on during your visit. The observatory is nearly on the equator so well placed for seeing both northern and southern constellations; there are free stargazing sessions every Friday evening.

THE BASICS

www.science.edu.sg
b3, arrowed off at A7
15 Science Centre Road
6425 2500
Daily 10–6
Café in SSC, fast food in Omni-Theatre
Jurong East then 500yd/m walk (turn left from station, along Block 135) or bus 335
66, 178, 198 direct; 51, 78, 197 to Jurong East Interchange then 335 or walk
Good
Inexpensive

Singapore Zoo and River Safari

TOP 25

HIGHLIGHTS

- "Open" enclosures
- Tigers and Bengal White
- Pygmy hippos
- Primate islands
- Air-conditioned shelters
- Treetops Trail
- Komodo dragons
- Children's World
- Tram
- River Safari

TIP

- Consider a Park Hopper 3-in-1 ticket for the zoo, Night Safari and Jurong Bird Park.

The award-winning zoo has been offering animal lovers the opportunity to observe a wide range of wildlife since the 1970s. River Safari, opened in 2013, is inspired by iconic rivers from around the world.

The zoo Singapore's zoo, acclaimed as one of the finest in the world, is also one of the youngest. Its beginnings can be traced back to the 1960s, when British forces pulled out of Singapore and left a ragbag of family pets behind. The zoo, which sprawls over 69 acres (28 hectares), was officially opened in 1973 and is now home to more than 300 species, some endangered and rare, such as tigers, orangutans, Komodo dragons and golden lion tamarins, kept in as natural conditions as possible. Breeding programs have been initiated for

Clockwise from left: kangaroo feeding time; a giraffe; the tiger enclosure is one of the highlights; a young orangutan; freshwater aquarium at River Safari; feeding time with the orangutans

endangered species, with some success. A tram (extra charge) trundles round the grounds to save you some walking.

River Safari This S$160-million attraction is Asia's first river-themed safari park. The ambitious concept is divided into different zones dedicated to the Mississippi, Congo, Nile, Ganges, Murray, Mekong and Yangtze rivers—guests stroll through the park and encounter wildlife native to these bodies of water. The park is also home to Southeast Asia's largest panda exhibit, home of Kai Kai and Jia Jia, and the world's largest freshwater aquarium. Make sure to take a ride on the Amazon River Quest, a boat adventure that floats past over 30 species of animals, including giant anteaters and jaguars. Be prepared: you will get wet!

THE BASICS

www.zoo.com.sg
www.riversafari.com.sg
c2, arrowed off at D1
80 Mandai Lake Road
6269 3411
Zoo daily 8.30–6. River Safari daily 9–6
Restaurants
Ang Mo Kio, then SBS bus 138, or Choa Chu Kang then TIBS 927
SBS bus 171 to Mandai Road then cross road and take 138 or 927
Good
Expensive

More to See

CHINESE AND JAPANESE GARDENS

www.jtc.gov.sg

Chinese and Japanese classical gardens have been created on two islands in Jurong Lake. The Chinese Garden covers 32 acres (13 hectares) and is dotted with pagodas, pavilions and arched bridges. The main building is based on Beijing's Summer Palace. During the mid-autumn festival the gardens are hung with lanterns. The Bridge of Double Beauty leads to the Japanese Gardens, which are altogether more serene, and take their inspiration from gardens of the 15th to 17th centuries with their Zen rock gardens, shrubs, lanterns and ponds.

b3 1 Chinese Garden Road 6261 3632 Daily 6am–11pm Refreshment kiosks Chinese Garden Inexpensive

COLONIAL RESIDENCES

A walk along Cluny, Lermit and Nassim roads, between the west end of Orchard Road and the Botanic Gardens, will give glimpses of 19th-century colonial residences. These mansions come equiped for making living in the tropical heat as tolerable as possible: enormous blinds, shaded balconies and verandas, and lush, landscaped gardens.

c3, A3 Cluny, Lermit and Nassim roads Orchard Free

HARBOURFRONT

The HarbourFront precinct, which includes the Singapore Cruise Centre, spans 59 acres (24 hectares) along Singapore's southern waterfront at the foothills of Mount Faber, and overlooks the resort island of Sentosa (▷ 62). A popular destination, this former exhibition area has been transformed into a vibrant hub for work, living and recreation, and is a great place to come for waterfront dining and shopping at VivoCity (▷ 77), Singapore's largest mall. You can also pick up the panoramic cable car here to ride up to the top of Mount Faber or across to Sentosa.

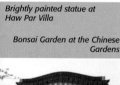

Brightly painted statue at Haw Par Villa

Bonsai Garden at the Chinese Gardens

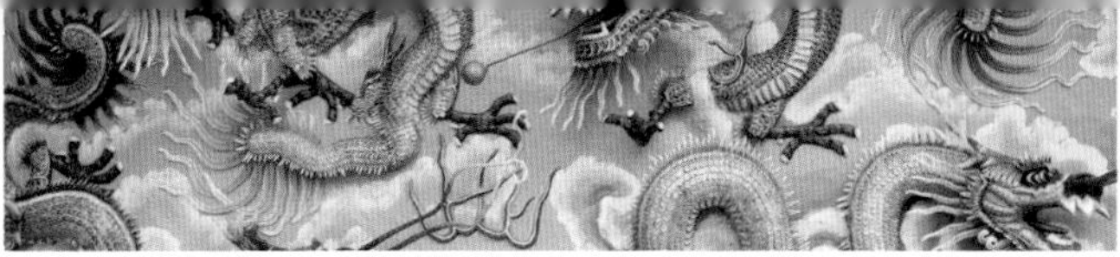

c4, B9 1 Maritime Square 7am–midnight daily HarbourFront

HAW PAR VILLA (TIGER BALM GARDENS)

Brothers Aw Boon Haw and Aw Boon Par built themselves a villa here in 1937 after making their fortune with Tiger Balm curative ointment. The house is no longer there, but the gardens are filled with tableaux of rather gaudy statues based on Chinese legends and real crimes in old Singapore. The Ten Courts of Hell exhibit depicts gory scenes of punishment handed out to evil-doers, such as disembowelment or being plunged into a giant wok of boiling oil.

c3 262 Pasir Panjang Road 6872 2780 Daily 9–7 Cafés Buona Vista, then bus 200 Free

KRANJI COUNTRYSIDE

www.kranjicountryside.com

The Kranji Countryside Association was formed in 2005 to promote the rural northwest of the island, opening farms up to the public so locals and visitors can find out more abbout where their food actually comes from. The association operates the Kranji Countryside Express Bus, which brings travelers from the Kranj MRT station to nearby farms and Sungei Buloh Nature Reserve. You can hop on and off the bus as many times as you like. There's also a Heritage Trail around the area, which takes in a number of historical sites. Come for a leisurely lunch at Bollywood Veggies, then spend the afternoon wandering through the 10 acres (4 hectares) of grounds, which also include a Food Museum.

b1 Bollywood Veggies, 100 Neo Tiew Road 6261 3632 Wed–Sun 9–6 Several farms have restaurants Kranji, then Kranji Countryside Express Bus Inexpensive

KRANJI WAR MEMORIAL

The War Memorial is dedicated to the service personnel from

Kranji War Memorial Cemetery

Malaya, India, Sri Lanka, Australia, New Zealand, Britain and Canada who died defending Singapore and Malaya against the Japanese during World War II. Two of Singapore's past presidents also lie here. More than 4,000 graves stand in rows along the well-kept lawns, and the names of those whose bodies were not recovered (more than 24,000) are inscribed on the sides of the memorial's 12 walls. The cemetery, a hospital burial ground during the occupation, became a military cemetery after the war.

b1 9 Woodlands Road Daily 7am–6pm Kranji SBS bus 170 from Rochor Road Free

MEMORIES AT OLD FORD FACTORY

www.moff.nas.sg

It was at this brand new car factory that, on 15 February 1942, Lt.-Gen. A. E. Percival, Commander of the British Forces in Singapore, surrendered to General Yamashita of the Japanese Army.

Soon after, Singapore was renamed Syonan-To (Light of the South) and for nearly four years the Japanese ruled Singapore. The art deco-style building, originally built as Ford's first assembly plant in Asia, is now refurbished as a gallery showing the exhibition "Syonan Years: Singapore Under Japanese Rule, 1942–1945."

The exhibition, curated by the National Archives of Singapore, provides the background of World War II in Malaya and describes the hardships people endured during the Occupation. The pathway leading to the building was the ceremonial route taken by the British forces on the day of the surrender, and you enter the exhibition gallery through a tunnel, starting at the historic Board Room, where the signing of the surrender took place. On display are archival photographs, oral history interviews, maps and artefacts from the era.

On the mezzanine floor is an AV cinema showing documentaries

Memories at Old Ford Factory

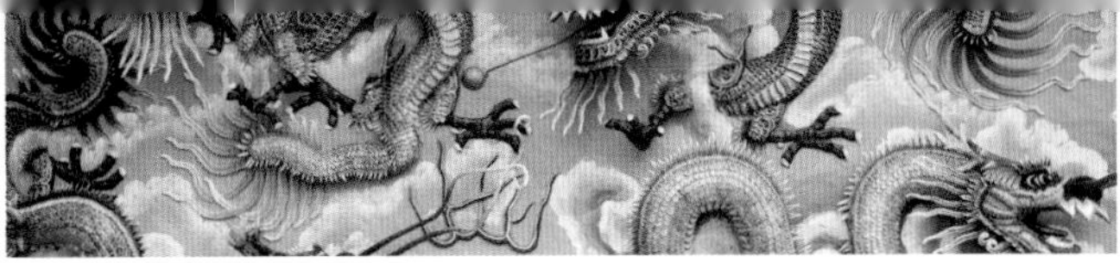

on various aspects of the Japanese Occupation and featuring exclusive footage from the depths of the archives.

In the grounds of the museum is a granite stone inscribed with a Tang dynasty verse entitled "Taking History as a Lesson" and a calligraphic sculpture called "He Ping" or Peace, which signifies the relief and calm that come at the end of war. Behind the old main wing is a garden plot planted with typical wartime crops, such as sugar cane and oil palm.

b2 · 351 Upper Bukit Timah Road · 6462 6724 · Mon–Sat 9–5.30, Sun 12–5.30 · Clementi, then SBS 184 · SBS Bus 170 · Reasonable · Inexpensive

NUS MUSEUM

www.nus.edu.sg/museum

The center manages Singapore National University's three art collections. The Chinese art collection, located at lobby level in the Lee Kong Chian Art Museum, has six galleries of paintings, calligraphy, ceramics and bronze objects representing every major era of China's long and illustrious history.

The South and Southeast Asian collection, at concourse level in the South and Southeast Asian Gallery, displays artworks that span classical to modern traditions in drawing and painting, textile, ceramics, sculptures and bronzes from around the region. Some of the works display historic traditions but there's plenty to keep fans of modern Asian art happy, including contemporary paintings, and textiles acquired during recent field trips.

The Ng Eng Teng collection, at the top level in the Ng Eng Teng Gallery, contains more than 1,000 items—sculptures, vessels, ceramic forms, paintings and drawings—by the eponymous Ng, Singapore's foremost sculptor (1934–2001).

b3 · University Cultural Centre Annex, 50 Kent Ridge Crescent, National University of Singapore · 6516 8817 · Tue–Sat 10–7.30, Sun 10–6 · Clementi, then bus 96 · Free

Exhibits in the NUS Centre for the Arts

Porcelain Buddha gilt-bronze mask, NUS Centre for the Arts

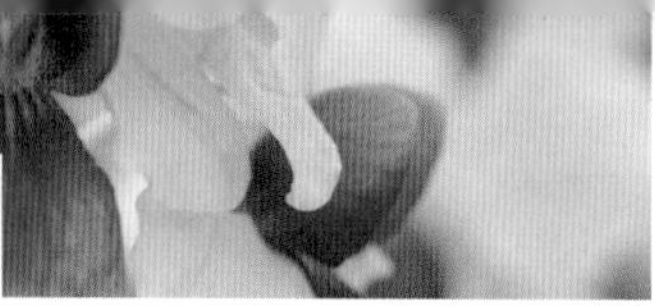

A walk through the Botanic Gardens

This walk takes you through the National Orchid Garden (▷ 56–57), so a good time to start is around opening hour—8.30am.

DISTANCE: 1–1.5 miles (1.5–2.5km) **ALLOW:** 2–3 hours

START

TANGLIN GATE (MAIN GATE)
A3, A4, 3 Botanic Gardens
7, 75, 105, 106, 123, 174

❶ Take the path to the left that leads to the March Garden ponds. These lovely ponds, created out of a natural wetlands, feature local and non-native water plants.

❷ Keep walking to the left around the ponds and follow some stepping stones. Take the turn to the right and walk along to Swan Lake, with its resident white swans and exuberant "Swing Me Mama" sculpture.

❸ Continue walking straight ahead until several paths meet and you can see three sets of steps. Take the middle steps to the Sundial Garden—you'll see a Floral Clock on the far side.

❹ Climb the steps to the left of the Floral Clock and turn left. Keep going and you'll reach the Sun Rockery, and a little farther on there is a display of the gorgeous Vanda "Miss Joaquim" orchid, the national flower of Singapore.

❺ When you reach the end of the orchid display, you'll see an extremely tall forest tree—walk down the path at its side and along to the Ginger Garden, home to plants in the ginger family and related species.

❻ A path from the Ginger Garden will take you directly to the Orchid Plaza and National Orchid Garden. Turn right once you're inside the gardens and walk to the fountain. Turn left here and walk uphill to the Tan Hoon Siang Misthouse.

❼ Down the hill to the right you'll find a huge collection of bromeliads, and the Cool House nearby that houses tropical montane orchid species. From here you loop back up to the Orchidarium, with its lowland species.

❽ Walk downhill to leave the Orchid Gardens. Stroll down the lawn at Palm Valley and admire the palms, then relax by Symphony Lake, before walking up to the Visitor Centre.

END

TANGLIN GATE OR VISITOR CENTRE

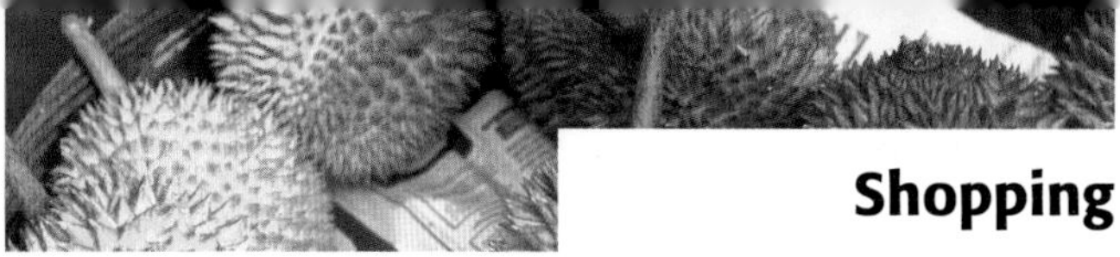

Shopping

ANTIQUES OF THE ORIENT

www.aoto.com.sg

You could spend hours browsing through this shop's fine selection of old lithographs, prints, maps and books.

B4 02-40 Tanglin Shopping Centre, 19 Tanglin Road 6734 9351 Mon–Sat 10–6, Sun 11–4 Orchard

ASIATIQUE COLLECTION

www.asiatiquecollections.com

A Dempsey Hill shop displaying modern and vintage jewelry, home accessories and art from around the region.

A4 14a Dempsey Road 6471 3146 Daily 11–7

HOLLAND ROAD SHOPPING CENTRE

Ethnic arts and crafts from all over Asia.

A4 211 Holland Avenue 6338 8135 Daily 10–9 Holland Village 5, 7, 61, 10

LIM'S ARTS & LIVING

www.lims.com.sg

Authentic handicrafts, including linens, jewelry, pottery and silk pyjamas.

A4 02–01 Holland Road Shopping Centre, 211 Holland Avenue 6467 1300 Daily 9.30–8.30 Holland Village

RESORTS WORLD SENTOSA LUXURY FASHION GALLERIA

Forming a linkway between three of Resorts World Sentosa's major hotels, luxury jewelers, watch-making brands and leading fashion houses line this 30,000sq ft (2,800sq m) stretch of high-end retail space.

A9 8 Sentosa Gateway 6723 8000 Daily 11–10.30 Harbourfront, then Sentosa Express

TANGLIN MALL

www.tanglinmall.com.sg

This shopping mall provides something a little different from the designer labels on offer elsewhere on Orchard Road. The range of stores includes some interesting children's shops, a sports shop and three floors of Food Junction.

B4 163 Tanglin Road 6736 4922 Daily 10–10 Orchard

CARPET AUCTIONS

Taking in a carpet auction can be a fun way to spend a Sunday. Several carpet companies hold auctions then, usually at the Hyatt, the Hilton or the Holiday Inn. Carpets are spread out for easy viewing from about 10 until just after noon. Estimated market prices are posted and a Continental-type buffet breakfast is often free to participants. Auctions usually start about 1. Depending on the number of viewers and the size of their wallets, bidding proceeds at a fast pace. Expect to get 50–70 percent off the estimated price, or at least start the bidding there.

TANGLIN SHOPPING CENTRE

www.tanglinsc.com

One of the area's oldest shopping malls, this is known for Asian antiques and curios (though, as elsewhere in Singapore, prices are high). It is also good for carpets, tailoring, cameras and accessories. Near the intersection of Tanglin and Orchard roads.

B4 19 Tanglin Road 6737 0849 Mon–Sat 12–6 Orchard

TERESE JADE & MINERALS

Jade is a Chinese favorite. Check out the loose beads and stones—you can make your own jewelry or have it custom made on the premises.

B4 01–28 Tanglin Shopping Centre, 19 Tanglin Road 6734 0379 Mon–Sat 10.30–6.30 Orchard

VIVOCITY

www.vivocity.com.sg

Singapore's biggest mall is a stunning retail and leisure complex on the waterfront, with department stores (including Tangs) and brand-name shops, plus restaurants, cinemas and a hypermarket.

B9 1 Harbourfront Walk C6377 6860 Daily 10–10 HarbourFront

Restaurants

PRICES

Prices are approximate, based on a 3-course meal for one person.
$$$ over S$50
$$ S$20–S$50
$ under S$20

DEMPSEY HILL ($–$$$)

www.dempseyhill.com

Tucked away near the Botanic Gardens, these former army barracks are now home to some of the city's top restaurants. Dine on the city's signature chili crabs at Long Beach, then enjoy a nightcap at the RedDot Brew House.

Off map A4 Dempsey Road Times vary

LA FORKETTA ($$$)

www.laforketta.com.sg

The food at this Italian restaurant is delicious, particularly the pizza.

Off map A4 01-09 Dempsey Hill, 9 Dempsey Road 6475 2298 Mon–Fri 12–2.30, 6–10.30, Sat–Sun 11.30–2.30, 6–10.30

MICHELANGELO'S ($$)

www.michelangelos.com.sg

Innovative Italian cuisine from this award-winning restaurant comes in generous portions served by professional staff. Dine among the frescoes or eat outside by candlelight.

A4 01–60 Chip Bee Gardens, Block 44 Jalan Merah Saga 6475 9069 Mon–Sun 11.30–2.30, 5.30–10.30 Holland Village

O'COFFEE CLUB ($)

www.ocoffeeclub.com

The O'Coffee Club chain specializes in interesting coffees, some with cream and a choice of spirits. Also a selection of pastas, salads and sandwiches.

A4 48 Lorong Mambong 6466 0296 Mon–Thu 11am–midnight, Fri–Sat 11am–1am, Sun 10am–midnight Holland Village

ORIGINAL SIN ($$)

www.originalsin.com.sg

The menu at this Mediterranean-style restaurant is completely vegetarian. The imaginative use of ingredients gives run-of-the-mill dishes a real twist.

Off map to west 01–62 Chip Bee Gardens, Block 43, Jalan Merah Saga, Holland Village 6475 5605 Daily 11.30–2.30, 6–10.30 Holland Village

COFFEE SHOPS

Singapore's traditional coffee shops are nothing like the modern places that sell a sophisticated selection of lattes and pastries. They are no-nonsense, cheap and cheerful options for popular local rice and noodle dishes. You also get coffee, locally referred to as *"kopi"*, but it's thick and sweet, made with condensed milk. Mindful of waste, coffee shops sometimes serve takeout coffee in empty condensed-milk cans, and you will occasionally see people carrying these, though the more usual coffee container today is the familiar Styrofoam container or a plastic bag, which you can sometimes see tied to railings while the contents cool.

ROCHESTER PARK ($$$)

This trendy dining district, close to Holland Village, has several smart restaurants in colonial bungalows. Choices include Chinese, Continental and Italian. Expensive, quality food.

A4 Rochester Park Buena Vista 74, 91, 92, 95, 191, 196

ROCKY'S ($$)

If you feel like ordering pizza to eat in, Rocky's is the place. Allow about an hour for delivery.

Off map to north Block 106, 12 Clementi Street 6468 9188 Daily 11–10.30 (last order 10)

SAMY'S CURRY ($)

www.samyscurry.com

Located in a former civil-service clubhouse, with a colonial edifice and overhead fans; meals here are served on banana leaves. Try spoonfuls of zesty curries, fragrant rices, breads and assorted condiments.

A4 25 Dempsey Road 6472 2080 Daily 11–3, 6–10

East Island

The east of Singapore boasts long, sandy beaches lined with excellent seafood restaurants, recreational water sports, including a cable ski park, poignant World War II memorials and historic temples.

MAL
Johor
Pulau Seletar
Pulau Punggol Barat
Yishun Park
Seletar Airport
Orchid Country Club
Lower Seletar Reservoir
TAMPINES
SELETAR EXPRESSWAY
YIO CHU KANG ROAD
CENTRAL EXPRESSWAY
YIO CHU KANG ROAD
ANG MO KIO
Yio Chu Kang
ANG MO KIO
ROAD
Ang Mo Kio
Kong Meng San Phor Kark See Temple
BISHAN
ANG MO KIO AVE
SERANGOON
Lorong Chuan
Bishan
MARYMOUNT
Marymount
BRADDELL ROAD
SERANGOON
Caldecott
Braddell
TOA PAYOH
Siong Lim Temple
UPPER
Woodleigh
Potong Pasir
Toa Payoh
Central Sikh TempleV
Boon Keng
Aljunied
Kallang
Singapore Sports Hub
Stadium
MARINA COASTAL EXPRESSWAY
Jurong
Pandan
Sentosa
Pulau Busing
Pulau Bukom
Pulau Tekukor
Pulau Seringat
Pulau Jong
Pulau Sakijang Bendera
St John's Island
Pulau Tembakul
Kusu Island
Pulau Sudong
Pulau Semakau
Pulau Sebarok
Pulau Darat
Pulau Subar Laut
Pulau Sakijang Pelepah
Lazarus
1
2
3
4
b
c

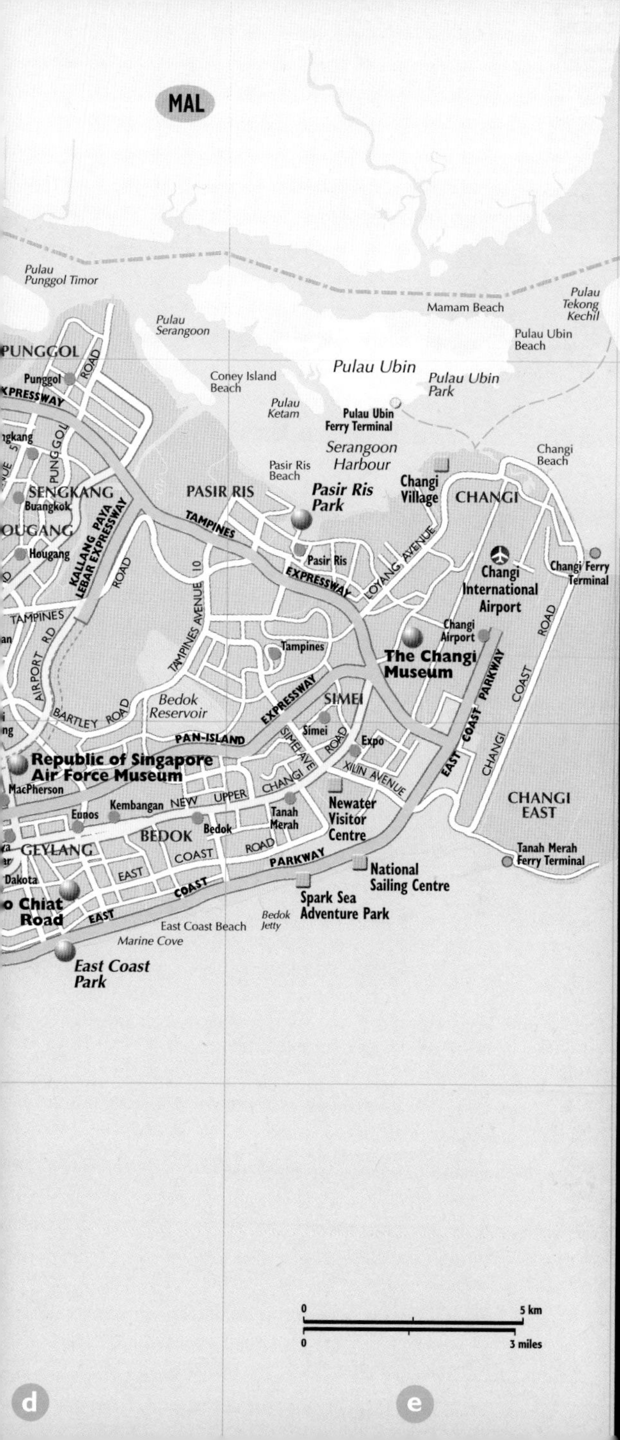
MAL
Pulau Punggol Timor
Pulau Serangoon
Mamam Beach
Pulau Tekong Kechil
Pulau Ubin Beach
PUNGGOL
Punggol
EXPRESSWAY
ROAD
Coney Island Beach
Pulau Ubin
Pulau Ubin Park
Pulau Ketam
Pulau Ubin Ferry Terminal
PUNGGOL
Serangoon Harbour
Changi Beach
Pasir Ris Beach
SENGKANG
Buangkok
PASIR RIS
Pasir Ris Park
Changi Village
CHANGI
HOUGANG
KALLANG PAYA LEBAR EXPRESSWAY
TAMPINES
Hougang
ROAD
TAMPINES AVENUE 10
Pasir Ris
LOYANG AVENUE
Changi International Airport
Changi Ferry Terminal
EXPRESSWAY
TAMPINES
RD
AIRPORT
Tampines
Changi Airport
ROAD
The Changi Museum
EAST COAST PARKWAY
COAST
Bedok Reservoir
BARTLEY ROAD
EXPRESSWAY
SIMEI
PAN-ISLAND
Simei
SIMEI AVE
ROAD
Expo
CHANGI
Republic of Singapore Air Force Museum
MacPherson
XILIN AVENUE
CHANGI
Kembangan
NEW
UPPER
CHANGI
Newater Visitor Centre
CHANGI EAST
Eunos
Tanah Merah
Bedok
BEDOK
GEYLANG
COAST
ROAD
PARKWAY
Tanah Merah Ferry Terminal
Dakota
EAST
National Sailing Centre
COAST
Joo Chiat Road
EAST
Spark Sea Adventure Park
East Coast Beach
Bedok Jetty
Marine Cove
East Coast Park
0
5 km
0
3 miles
d
e

The Changi Museum

TOP 25

The Changi Chapel (left) and the museum chapel memorial wall (right)

THE BASICS

www.changimuseum.com
e2
1000 Upper Changi Road North
6214 2451
Daily 9.30–5
Tanah Merah, then SBS bus 2
Free

HIGHLIGHTS

- Replica Murals
- Video screenings
- Wartime plants

During World War II, some 50,000 civilians, Allied troops and prisoners were incarcerated in Singapore. The Changi Museum portrays the terrible conditions they endured—some for more than three years.

Fitting memorial Housed within the open-air courtyard of the museum, the Changi Chapel is a reconstruction of one of the many chapels built at Changi Prison during the Japanese Occupation. This poignant monument to those who strived to maintain their faith during their years in captivity is a fitting memorial to all who were imprisoned.

Changi Murals The museum displays photographs, letters, drawings and personal effects of some of the tens of thousands of civilians, soldiers and other war prisoners. There is also a replica of the original Changi Murals, which were painted by bombardier Stanley Warren. Visitors are welcome to join the 9am Sunday services, conducted by various church groups at the Changi Chapel.

"Elizabeth Choy" There are regular screenings of short films such as "Changi Through The Eyes of Haxworth" about a prisoner whose sketches vividly capture his years in Changi, and "Elizabeth Choy," the story of a civilian heroine who withstood nearly 200 days of imprisonment and torture. Visitors can take 45-minute guided tours or venture out on their own with an audio tour. There is a café and the garden has a collection of plants that Singapore residents typically planted during the Japanese Occupation.

A shop display on Joo Chiat Road (left) and terraced houses (right)

TOP 25

Joo Chiat Road

Original architecture and intriguing old businesses by day, and an exciting mix of restaurants and music lounges in the evening, give a fascinating glimpse of former times and a sample of Singapore life today.

History This once quiet seaside village is today an eclectic mix of colonial villas, Peranakan-style terraces and Malay bungalows. Some are preserved, many are being renovated, others remain untouched. The Joo Chiat Complex, at the northern end of Joo Chiat near the Malay Village, is a busy local shopping complex selling fabrics and household goods at bargain prices. Next to the Village is the Geylang Serai market (▷ 90), a traditional Asian market and a good place to browse.

Ecletic mix Opposite Guan Hoe Soon Restaurant (which serves traditional Peranakan *nonya* dishes) is a typical 1920s corner terrace, with an ornate frieze of green dragons on the roof pediment. Terrace houses with covered walkways can be found along the road. The second floors may be pillared verandas, or have ornate casement windows. Colorful tiles are another common feature. Koon Seng Road has two rows of terraced houses with courtyard gardens in front and extravagant moldings, tiles and paintwork.

New shops on the block The ongoing renovation of local shophouses and the construction of several condos nearby has led to the introduction of trendier shops, bars and restaurants, like Immigrants Gastrobar and Sinpopo Brand.

THE BASICS

- d3
- Joo Chiat Road
- Guan Hoe Soon 6344 2761 Katong Antique House 6345 8544
- Plentiful choice
- Paya Lebar then walk
- 16, 33
- None
- Free

HIGHLIGHTS

- Guan Hoe Soon Restaurant
- Joo Chiat Complex
- Katong Antique House
- Koon Seng Road
- Malay Village
- Malay-style bungalows
- Old seafront luxury villas
- Peranakan-style shophouses
- Residential terraces

East Coast Park

TOP 25

HIGHLIGHTS

- Big Splash
- Kayak rental
- East Coast Sailing Centre
- SKI360°
- Mana Mana
- Xtreme Skate Park

TIP

- Singapore's freshest seafood can be found at the waterfront eateries, but avoid Sunday, when they are always packed.

Two decades of land reclamation have created this beachside playground. Swim or sail; walk, jog or cycle the 6 miles (10km) of tracks between coconut groves; or laze on white sands.

Plenty to do Picnicking families flock to the area on the weekends. There are many places to rent a bicycle, canoe or rollerblades, and it's a pleasant place to relax and catch a cooling breeze in the evening. The East Coast Seafood Centre is popular with those who appreciate excellent seafood, but it is only open in the evening and loses some of the beach ambience amid a large concrete plaza. The East Coast Lagoon Food Village farther east is another popular spot, and feels slightly more down to earth and natural.

Clockwise from left: a beach scene at East Coast Park; a lone bicycle on the beach; enjoying a picnic bbq; the cable ski park; you can also rent bicycles here

Outdoor adventures East Coast Park is perfect for anyone looking to take advantage of the warm weather year round. Water-sport enthusiasts can stop by Mana Mana to rent equipment for windsurfing, stand-up paddle boarding or kayaking out in the ocean. SKI360°, a cable ski park, is set up nearby—the overhead cable pulls wakeboarders across the water at speeds up to 37mph (60kph). Xtreme Skate Park is a great spot to watch ambitious skateboarders and bikers conquer impressive bowls. Those traveling with tots in tow should stop by Big Splash, where you'll find an indoor mini golf course modeled after Singapore landmarks.

Beaches The 12 miles (20km) of beaches are popular on weekends, but swimming in the often murky waters is not advised.

THE BASICS

www.nparks.gov.sg

d3, J5 to M5

East Coast Service Road

ECSC 6449 5118. Big Splash 6345 1321. SKI360° 6442 7318

East Coast Lagoon Food Centre and Jumbo Seafood (n92), various kiosks, fast food at Marina Cove and Big Splash

Bedok, then bus 401 or bus 31, 197; Eunos, then 55, 155; Paya Lebar, then 76, 135 and walk

16, 31, 55, 76, 135, 155, 196, 197, 853 daily to Marine Parade Road; 401 to East Coast Service Road (Sun)

Some level paths

Free; rental charges per hour for sports, etc

More to See

BETEL BOX

www.betelbox.com

As well as serving as a reliable hostel, playing host to many a backpacker over the years, Betel Box also began the Real Singapore Tours. One of the most popular is the Joo Chiat/Katong Food Walk, where visitors are led through some of the best local eateries, being introduced to Singaporean cuisine and taught about local customs. They also offer several bike tours, nature walks and even a pub crawl. All tours begin at the Betel Box hostel on Joo Chiat Road.

d3 200 Joo Chiat Road 6247 7340 Days and times vary Paya Lebar Prices vary

BISHAN HDB ESTATE

More than 80 percent of Singapore's population lives in state-subsidized Housing and Development Board apartments (HDBs). Hundreds of these government-built blocks exist in any given area, each a small town in its own right. Bishan was developed in the early 1990s. As with most HDB areas, it has its own MRT station, around which a shopping and entertainment complex, Junction 8, has been built. Wander around Junction 8's central area, up Bishan Road, and from there turn right in front of the MRT, then left into Street 22. You'll come upon one of the many smaller satellite areas, complete with its own shops and hawker center at the base of the housing blocks. On the outskirts of Bishan, at Bright Hill Drive, is Phor Kark See, a huge Buddhist temple overlooking Bishan Park.

c2 Bishan Central 3rd Mini Steamboat Delight, 9 Bishan Place, 04–01G and numerous other coffee shops, hawker centers and fast-food outlets Bishan 13, 53, 54, 55, 56, 156 Few Free

PASIR RIS PARK

This 175-acre (71-hectare) area lying at the end of the East-West MRT line contains some of Singapore's last remaining stretches of mangrove swamp, and is now a bird and nature reserve. Raised boardwalks meander

Bishan HDB Estate

through this habitat. Look for fiddler crabs, mudskippers and small-clawed otters. Birds you might spot include herons, yellow-vented bulbuls, brown-throated sunbirds and collared kingfishers. You can also walk or cycle direct to East Coast Park from here along the new connecting path.
e2 Off Jalan Loyang Kecil 24 hours Pasir Ris, then bus 403 Free

REPUBLIC OF SINGAPORE AIR FORCE MUSEUM

www.mindef.gov.sg/rsaf/about/te-afm.asp
This museum allows close-up inspection of a wide range of aircraft, from an early Cessna to the more recent A4-S Skyhawk. On the first level, the museum has a "History of Aviation" exhibition, while upstairs are eight indoor galleries where you'll learn about the history of the RSAF, see models of past and present aircraft, radar and weapons systems, and an interactive model of the Tengah Air Base. Gallery 4 features a Bloodhound missile and an interactive model of the Launch Control Post. Would-be pilots will enjoy the Flight Simulator in Gallery 5. The presentation is highly interactive, with multimedia displays.
d3 400 Airport Road 6461 8504/8506 Tue–Sun 8.30–5 Cafeteria SBS 90 and 94 (SBS 90 not available on Sun) Free

SIONG LIM TEMPLE

Set amid HDB residential towers, the Siong Lim Temple is a national monument to Singapore's Chinese immigrants, built between 1868 and 1908 and renovated in 2002. The architecture incorporates elements of the building styles of Fujian province, in southeast China, from where the original laborers came. The seven-floor gold-topped pagoda is a replica of the one at the 800-year-old Shanfeng temple in Fujian. The oldest building, a small wooden shrine, contains murals of the much-loved Chinese legend "Journey to the West."
d3 184E Jalan Toa Payoh 6259 6924 Daily 6.30am–9pm Toa Payoh Free

Pasir Ris Park mangrove boardwalk

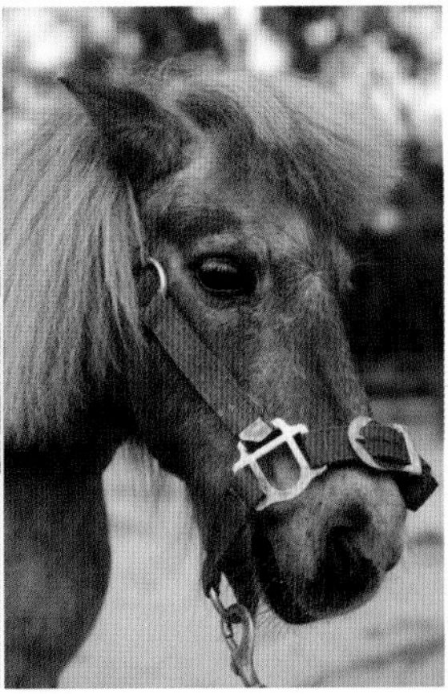

Pony rides at Pasir Ris Park

East Coast Park Walk

This recreational park (▷ 84–85) running for 12 miles (20km) along the East Coast, has water sports and seafood restaurants.

DISTANCE: 1–1.5 miles (1.5–2.5km) **ALLOW:** 2–3 hours

START

BUS STOP

e3 Bedok then 401, or 31, 197; Eunos then 55, 155, 196 to Marine Crescent and Marine Terrace

1 Walk to the lagoon, where you can watch cable-skiers of all ages practice their wakeboarding skills at SKI360°. Bring your bathing suit and have a go!

2 When you're finished, head north up the beach to the East Coast Lagoon Food Centre, a popular hawker area, for a cool, fresh tropical fruit drink and an exotic snack.

3 Continue on up the beach to the nearby Mana Mana and rent a paddle board or kayak, or just sit in the shade and watch the action.

4 If there's not much wind, you can rent a dinghy a bit farther up the beach and row to the nearby Bedok Jetty, which is popular with recreational fisherfolk.

5 By now you should have worked up a real appetite, so head south down the beach to the East Coast Seafood Centre, where there are many restaurants specializing in seafood. Try the local favorites—crispy baby octopus, drunken prawns and chilli crab—wonderful!

6 Take a walk farther down the beach or a quiet nap under a beach-side coconut tree before you return to the bus stop for the trip back to the Bedok Interchange.

END

BUS STOP

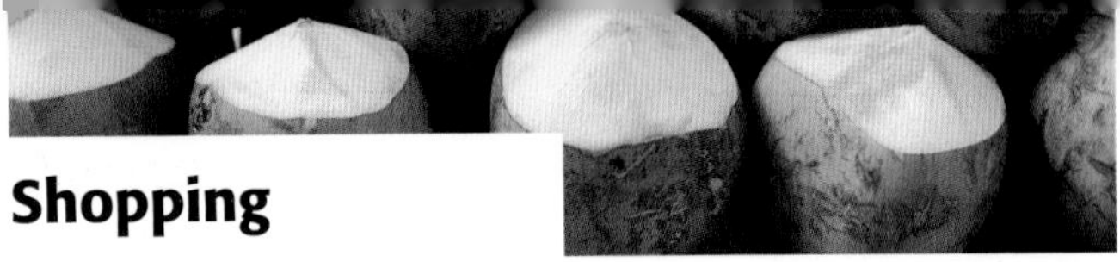

Shopping

112 KATONG

www.112katong.com.sg

Located at the intersection of East Coast and Joo Chiat roads, the six levels include over 150 shops, as well as a roof garden with a wet playground for kids.

M4 112 East Coast Road 6636 2112 Daily 10–10 Paya Lebar, then free shuttle bus 10, 10E, 12, 14, 14E, 16, 32, 40

BANGKU BANGKU

This furniture shop is filled with beautiful pieces shipped in from Indonesia. In addition to large chests, chairs and lamps, they also sell smaller, easily transportable items like doorknobs and retro antiques from the 1950s and 80s.

M3 317 Joo Chiat Road 8206 2946 Sat–Wed 11–9, Fri 2–9 Eunos 16, 33

BUGIS JUNCTION

www.bugisjunction-mall.com.sg

An interesting glass-covered shopping street with shophouses, modern retail outlets and a movie theater.

F5 200 Victoria Street 6557 6557 Bugis

BUGIS STREET

www.bugis-street.com

The simple clothes, accessory and shoe stalls in the largest street shopping venue in Singapore attracts hordes of bargain hunters. You can also pick up a fresh fruit juice or enjoy cheap fish.

F5 4 New Bugis Street 6338 9513 Daily 11–10 Bugis

CENTURY SQUARE AND TAMPINES MALL

www.centurysquare.com.sg

These malls are hugely popular with Tampines residents and convenient for a last-minute splurge before leaving from Changi Airport.

e2 2-4 Tampines Central 6789 6261; 6788 8370 Tampines

CHANGI VILLAGE

Specialty shops in a village atmosphere. Everything at bargain prices: electronic equipment, shoes, batik dresses, Indian cotton clothing, kimonos, and carpets.

e2 North of Changi Airport Tanah Merah, then take SBS bus no.2

ANTIQUES

Furniture and objects more than 100 years old, considered antiques, are sold in a plethora of antiques and reproduction shops. Buy only from reputable dealers. They will give a certificate of antiquity or a detailed description along with a receipt. This proof may be required to ensure duty-free importation to the US and UK. Prices are usually lower in the country of origin than in Singapore; they vary widely here, and bargaining is essential.

GEYLANG SERAI

Located in Geylang, this is the cultural heart of the Malay community in Singapore. The buildings house restaurants and shops specializing in traditional Malay cuisine, textiles and crafts. The area is free to wander around.

d3 Geylang Serai 6294 7559 Daily 10–10 Paya Lebar

RUMAH BEBE

www.rumahbebe.com

Discover new bits of Peranakan history in this shophouse, dedicated to the preservation of traditional arts and showcasing this unique culture. Browse the brightly colored selection of clothing, shoes and accessories, or take a tour.

M4 113 East Coast Road 6247 8781 Tue–Sun 9.30–6.30 10, 10E, 12, 14, 14E, 16, 32, 40

SIM LIM SQUARE

www.simlimsquare.com.sg

Several floors of shops sell electronic goods, including domestic appliances, computers, software and televisions. Look for the red star that indicates a "Good Retailer" approved by the STB (▷ 11).

F5 1 Rochor Canal Road 6336 3922 Daily 10.30–9 Bugis

Entertainment and Nightlife

CHANGI SAILING CLUB

www.csc.org.sg

Although a private club and a long way out of town, this makes a lovely, relaxing place for an evening drink and meal on the small balcony overlooking the beach, under the palm trees or in the comfortable bar. Nonmembers are admitted for a dollar Monday to Friday evenings.

e3 32 Netheravon Road 6545 2876 Restaurant: daily 10–10 Tampines, then bus 29

THE CIDER PIT

In a city where the cost of beer is typically high and the variety limited, this bar along Joo Chiat Road, with over 40 beers and a wide selection of cider, is a great addition. Traditional British pub food is also available.

M4 328 Joo Chiat Road 6440 0504 Mon–Fri 5pm–1am, Sat–Sun 1pm–1am Eunos 16, 33

DOWNTOWN EAST

www.downtowneast.com.sg

This giant theme park-cum-resort has lots of entertainment choices at affordable prices: food courts, retail shopping, gaming areas and a children's play area.

e2 Pasir Ris Drive 3, next to Pasir Ris Park 6589 1688 Sun–Thu 10am–12.30am, Fri–Sat 10am–2.30am Pasir Ris, then take shuttle bus

INDIAN DANCE

www.nas.org.sg

Singapore's Indian population takes its dance very seriously, and local dance academies put on public performances. The exacting steps and hand gestures, the exciting rhythms and the brilliant costumes of dance forms such as *orissi* are an unusual delight and well worth checking out.

Nrityalaya Aesthetics Society F5 Stamford Arts Centre, 155 Waterloo Street 6336 6537 Bugis

JOO CHIAT ROAD

The southerly section of this famous old strip is a fabulous place to sample the laid-back and casual side to Singapore nightlife, from cold beers on fold-away pavement tables to karaoke and girlie bars. It's sleazy in parts, but safe and a refreshing change from the super trendy downtown establishments. Head for the junction with East Coast Road.

d3 Joo Chiat Road, junction with East Coast Road Daily from dusk Paya Labar, then walk or take a taxi

DANCE CLUBS

As in most cities, Singapore dance clubs tend to suit particular groups of revelers. While the older expat crowds can be found at bars along Boat Quay such as Harry's (▷ 48), the younger set tend to hang around Club Street and Ann Siang Hill at bars like La Terraza Rooftop Bar (▷ 49). Nightclubs like Kyo (▷ 48) and Zouk (▷ 49) attract both a local and international DJ-loving crowd.

MYRA'S BEACH CLUB

www.myrasbeachclub.com

Soak up the sea breeze with a margarita or mojito in hand at this beachside bar in East Coast Park.

Off map M5 1390 East Coast Road 6443 3005 Tue–Sun 11am–midnight 16, 31, 55, 76, 135, 155, 196, 197

SINGAPORE INDOOR STADIUM

www.sportshub.com.sg

This US$65 million stadium is home to many big sporting and live music events in Singapore. The ultramodern design includes a giant roof that resembles the Chinese character for the "lucky" number eight. Elton John, the Rolling Stones and the Harlem Globetrotters are among those who have played here.

d3 Stadium Walk 6344 2660 Check events 11, 16, 608

TAMPINES STADIUM ROCK CLIMBING WALL

This excellent climbing wall is one of the many in Singapore.

d2 25 Tampines Street 6781 1980 Daily 9am–11pm Tampines

Restaurants

PRICES

Prices are approximate, based on a 3-course meal for one person.
$$$ over S$50
$$ S$20–S$50
$ under S$20

CASA BOM VENTO ($$)

The trademark dish at this halal-certified Eurasian Peranakan restaurant is Devil's Curry. The atmosphere also pays tribute to the heritage, with old porcelain lampshades and marble tables.
M5 477 Joo Chiat Road 6440 0196
Tue–Sun 11.30–3, 5.30–9
Eunos 16, 33

EAST COAST LAGOON FOOD CENTRE ($)

Great food and sea breezes make this popular. The satay is very good, as are the laksa and seafood dishes, including chili or black pepper crab.
d3 East Coast Parkway
Late morning until late daily Bugis, then bus 401 (Sat, Sun, holidays only)

GUAN HOE SOON ($)

www.guanhosesoon.com
The oldest nonya restaurant in Singapore has been dishing out its house specials since 1953. Try the *ayam buah keluak*, chicken with nuts and a spicy sauce.
M3 38/40 Joo Chiat Place 6344 2761 Daily 11–3, 6–9.30 Eunos
10, 12, 14, 16, 32, 40

IMMIGRANTS GASTROBAR ($$)

www.immigrants-gastrobar.com
The retro-inspired setting is a great place to enjoy Eurasian-style tapas, including beef cheek rendang, chilled tofu with century egg and spicy chicken wings. Beer prices are decent and the whiskey menu is extensive.
M4 467 Joo Chiat Road 8511 7322 Daily 5pm–midnight Eunos
10, 12, 14, 16, 32, 40

JUMBO SEAFOOD ($$$)

Lots of tasty seafood dishes, but renowned for its chili crab.
d3 1208 East Coast Parkway 6442 3435
Daily 11.30–2, 6–11
Eunos, then bus 55 or 105
16, 55, 76, 135, 155

MANGO TREE ($$)

Popular beachside location and delicious southern Indian cuisine, plus sunset views.
d3 1000 East Coast Parkway 6442 8655
Daily 11.30–2.30, 6.30–11
Eunos, then bus 55 or 105
16, 55, 76, 135, 155

STEAMBOAT

Not a form of transportation, rather a delicious method of tableside cooking where a selection of fish, meat and vegetables is placed in a container of boiling broth; you can cook it exactly to your liking and retrieve it with chopsticks when it's achieved perfect readiness.

NO SIGNBOARD SEAFOOD ($$$)

www.nosignboardseafood.com
Originally a hawker stall with no signposting, the family-run brand has expanded to four sit-down branches. The Geylang location is a great spot to enjoy chili crab and fresh fish from the giant tanks.
K3 414 Geylang Road
6842 3415 Daily noon–1am Aljunied

SINPOPO BRAND ($)

Much of the look of this spot is inspired by the 1970s. The dishes are similar to what you would find in a hawker center, just in a much trendier, air-conditioned setting.
M4 458 Joo Chiat Road 6345 5034 Tue–Thu, Sun noon–10, Fri–Sat noon–midnight Eunos
10, 12, 14, 16, 32, 40

SKETCHES PASTA & WINE BAR ($)

Set around the kitchen, the idea of this friendly place is that you design your own pasta dishes from the list of fresh ingredients.
F5 200 Victoria Street, 01–85 Parco Bugis Junction
6339 8386 Daily 11–10 Bugis

Farther Afield

Singapore is so close to exciting Malaysian and Indonesian destinations that, if you have time, you should experience the exotic differences offered by some of the cities, ports and resorts of the area.

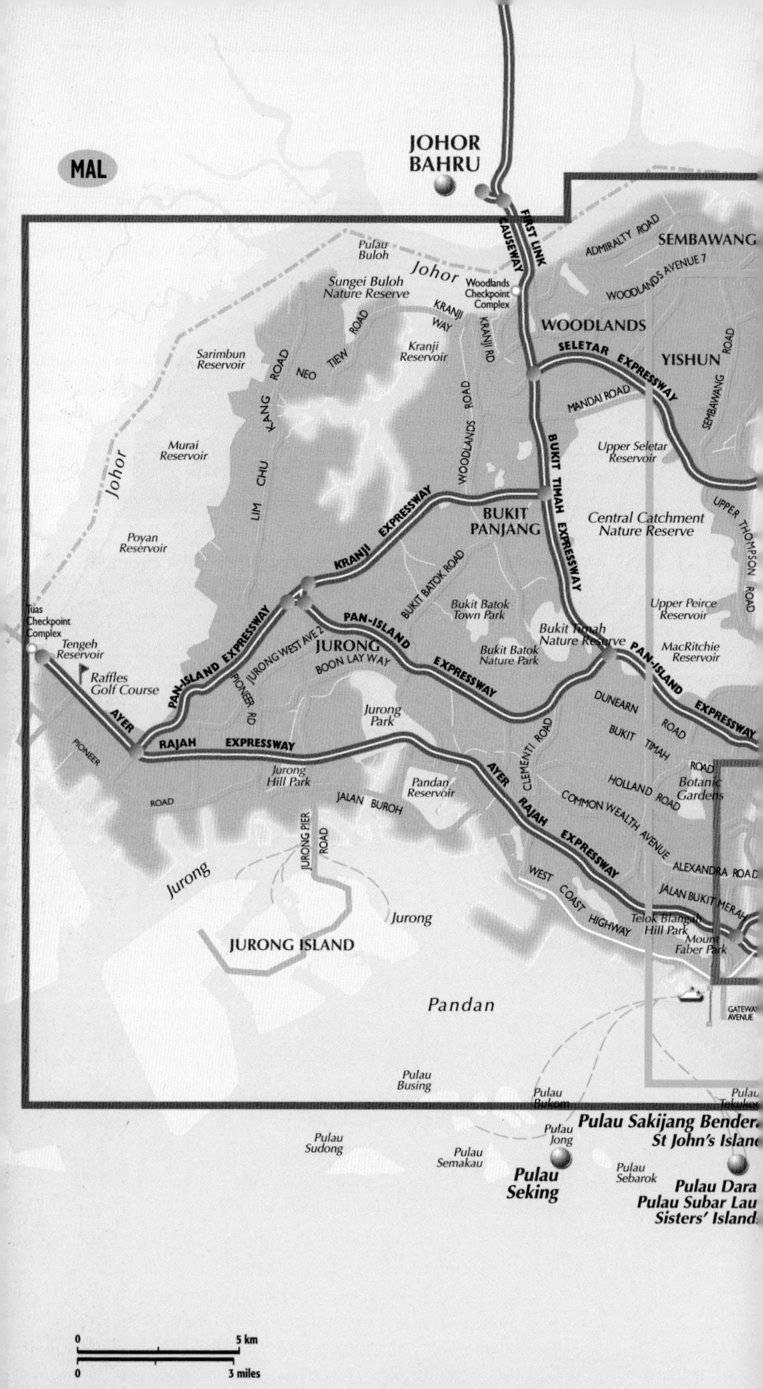
MAL
JOHOR BAHRU
FIRST LINK
CAUSEWAY
SEMBAWANG
ADMIRALTY ROAD
WOODLANDS AVENUE 7
Pulau Buloh
Johor
Woodlands Checkpoint Complex
Sungei Buloh Nature Reserve
KRANJI WAY
KRANJI RD
WOODLANDS
SELETAR EXPRESSWAY
YISHUN
SEMBAWANG ROAD
NEO TIEW ROAD
Kranji Reservoir
Sarimbun Reservoir
LIM CHU KANG ROAD
MANDAI ROAD
WOODLANDS ROAD
BUKIT TIMAH EXPRESSWAY
Upper Seletar Reservoir
Murai Reservoir
Johor
KRANJI EXPRESSWAY
BUKIT PANJANG
Central Catchment Nature Reserve
UPPER THOMPSON ROAD
Poyan Reservoir
BUKIT BATOK ROAD
Bukit Batok Town Park
Upper Peirce Reservoir
Tuas Checkpoint Complex
Tengeh Reservoir
Raffles Golf Course
PAN-ISLAND EXPRESSWAY
JURONG WEST AVE 2
JURONG
BOON LAY WAY
Bukit Timah Nature Reserve
MacRitchie Reservoir
Bukit Batok Nature Park
PIONEER RD
Jurong Park
DUNEARN ROAD
BUKIT TIMAH ROAD
AYER RAJAH EXPRESSWAY
CLEMENTI ROAD
PIONEER ROAD
Jurong Hill Park
Pandan Reservoir
HOLLAND ROAD
Botanic Gardens
JALAN BUROH
COMMON WEALTH AVENUE
JURONG PIER ROAD
ALEXANDRA ROAD
Jurong
WEST COAST HIGHWAY
JALAN BUKIT MERAH
Telok Blangah Hill Park
Mount Faber Park
JURONG ISLAND
Pandan
GATEWAY AVENUE
Pulau Busing
Pulau Bukom
Pulau Tekukor
Pulau Sakijang Bendera
St John's Island
Pulau Jong
Pulau Sudong
Pulau Semakau
Pulau Seking
Pulau Sebarok
Pulau Dara
Pulau Subar Laut
Sisters' Island
0
5 km
0
3 miles

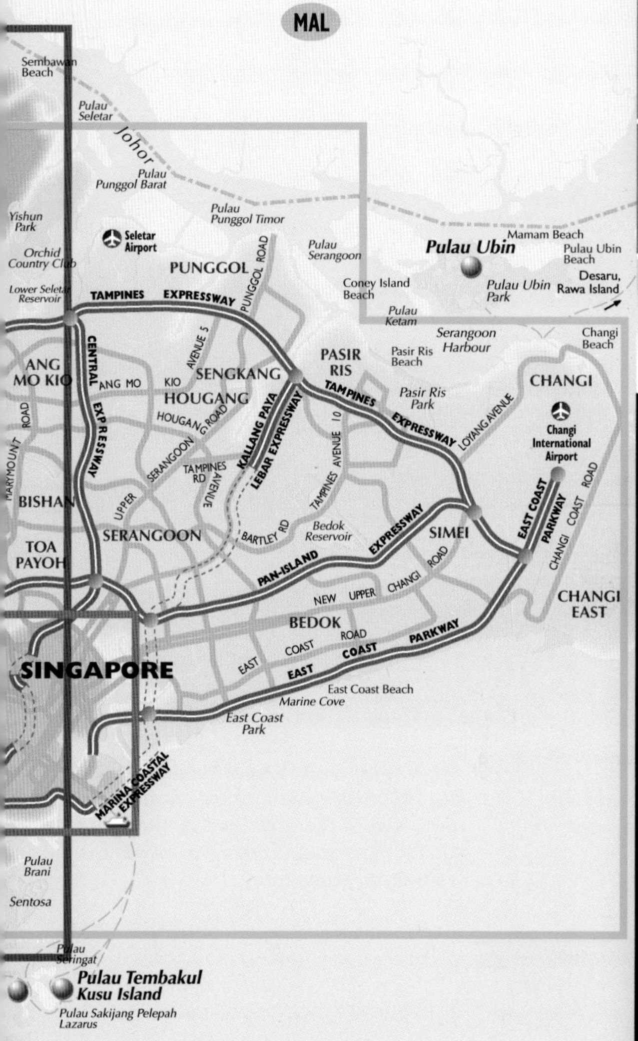
MAL
Sembawan Beach
Pulau Seletar
Johor
Pulau Punggol Barat
Pulau Punggol Timor
Yishun Park
Seletar Airport
Orchid Country Club
Lower Seletar Reservoir
PUNGGOL
PUNGGOL ROAD
Pulau Serangoon
Pulau Ubin
Mamam Beach
Pulau Ubin Beach
Desaru, Rawa Island
Pulau Ubin Park
Coney Island Beach
Pulau Ketam
Serangoon Harbour
Changi Beach
TAMPINES EXPRESSWAY
AVENUE 5
CENTRAL EXPRESSWAY
ANG MO KIO
ANG MO KIO
SENGKANG
HOUGANG
PASIR RIS
Pasir Ris Beach
Pasir Ris Park
CHANGI
Changi International Airport
LOYANG AVENUE
ROAD
MARYMOUNT
HOUGANG ROAD
SERANGOON
KALLANG PAYA LEBAR EXPRESSWAY
TAMPINES AVENUE 10
TAMPINES RD
AVENUE
TAMPINES
BISHAN
UPPER
SERANGOON
BARTLEY RD
Bedok Reservoir
EXPRESSWAY
SIMEI
EAST COAST PARKWAY
CHANGI COAST ROAD
TOA PAYOH
PAN-ISLAND
NEW UPPER CHANGI ROAD
CHANGI EAST
BEDOK
ROAD
EAST COAST
EAST COAST PARKWAY
SINGAPORE
East Coast Beach
Marine Cove
East Coast Park
MARINA COASTAL EXPRESSWAY
Pulau Brani
Sentosa
Pulau Seringat
Pulau Tembakul Kusu Island
Pulau Sakijang Pelepah Lazarus

Pulau Ubin

TOP 25

HIGHLIGHTS

- Groves of coconuts
- Old rubber plantation
- Mangrove swamps
- Hiking

TIP

- Be sure to take insect repellent and sunscreen, as well as a good hat.

Often compared to how Singapore was in the 1960s, this boomerang-shaped island northeast of the mainland is filled with coconut groves and mangrove swamps waiting to be explored.

Eating and drinking Just off the jetty at Pulau Ubin there is an endearingly scruffy little village where you can enjoy Malay and Chinese specialties. You have a choice of walking or renting a bicycle for some leisurely exploring. There are drink stalls scattered around the island, offering cold drinks as well as fresh coconuts. Pulau Ubin's many fruit orchards produce delicious durian, mangosteens and rambutans in season.

Wildlife and temples Keep an eye out for local bird life in the mangrove swamps and forests.

Clockwise from top left: fishing on Pulau Ubin; a local bungalow on the island; cycle tours are available on the island; Kelongs (wooden houses above the water on stilts) can still be seen on Pulau Ubin

Pulau Ubin is very poplular with bird-watchers. Several hornbills make their home on the island, as well as the red junglefowl, the wild ancestor of the domestic chicken. You can visit traditional temples and shrines as you make your way around the island. You'll find the Lotus Pond Temple just after the bridge over Sungei Jelutong. The pond near the temple is a beautiful sight when the flowers are in bloom.

Chek Jawa Any walk will take you by the sites of old limestone quarries, but Chek Jawa is the most visited coastal area on the island. Here you can explore the rocky shoreline, mangroves and beaches—look for the sand bar where you'll find starfish, crabs and sand dollars at low tide. You can also climb up the 65ft-high (20m) observation tower for fine views towards Malaysia.

THE BASICS

e2

Tampines, then bus 29 to Changi Village interchange. It's a 10-min bumboat ride from Changi Jetty (near the Changi Village Hawker Centre) to the jetty at Pulau Ubin. Bumboats operate from 6am to 11pm

Bumboat ticket inexpensive

Free guided walks organized by National Parks ☎ 6542 4108, 6545 4761

More to See

DESARU

www.myoutdoor.com

On the eastern tip of the Malaysian peninsula, Desaru is a popular beach resort for Singaporeans, and a good introduction to Malaysian culture. Its casuarina-lined, clean, sandy white beaches are fringed by lush tropical forest. There are numerous resorts and hotels—activities include golfing, horse riding, tennis, canoeing, swimming, boating, fishing and snorkeling.

Off map 78 miles (125km) northeast of Singapore. Accessible from Singapore by road via Kota Tinggi (2-hour drive), and by ferry from Changi Ferry Terminal, Mon–Thu, 3 times a day and Fri–Sun, 4 times a day 6546 8518

RAWA ISLAND

Within four hours of Singapore, this tropical private island off the east coast of Malaysia is popular for those looking for an escape from city life. Owned by sultan brothers who had different ideas on what to offer guests, the island is divided between Rawa Safaris Island Resort, a family-friendly place to stay with a dive center and waterslides; and laid-back Alang's Rawa, where guests will find bungalows on the beach with basic amenities and great home-cooked meals.

Off map 120 miles (194km) northeast of Singapore. Hotels will arrange 30-min boat transfer from Mersing, Malaysia Rawa Safaris Island Resort 607 235 1217; Alang's Rawa 6012 715 5547 Expensive

ST. JOHN'S ISLAND

Just 0.6 miles (1km) south of Sentosa, St. John's Island (formerly known as Pulau Sekijang Bendara) is a former penal settlement with idyllic, clean, sandy beaches, walking tracks and lagoons for swimming. The holiday bungalows, which can accommodate 10 people, have low rents and the picnic grounds are perfect for day-trippers.

c4 4 miles (6.5km) south of Singapore 45-min ferry ride from Marina South Pier. Departure times: Mon–Fri 10, 2, Sat 9, 12, 3, Sun 9, 11, 1, 3, 5 Expensive 6534 9339

St. John's Island

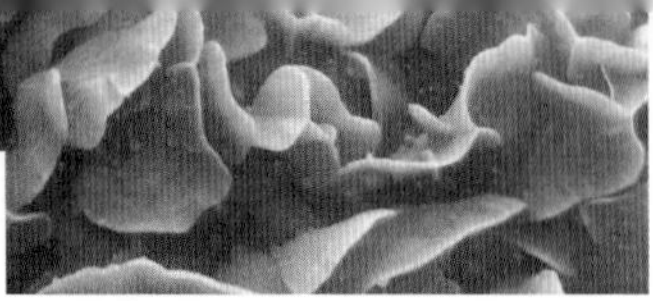

Diving Singapore's Islands

LEARN TO DIVE

Orpheus Dive Centre is a PADI 5-Star dive center offering scuba diving courses, ranging from beginner to professional levels. They offer "learning how to scuba dive" courses from S$350. Weekly classes are held in popular West Malaysian destinations such as Pulau Tioman and Pulau Dayang.
www.orpheusdive.com
☎ 66887 3631
✉ 16 Zion Road, Singapore

Some of Singapore's offshore islands are suitable for scuba diving, although due to often strong currents, divers should take organized tours. Local dive schools conduct NAUI or PADI courses with day and night diving options.

Kusu Island (Pulau Tembakul Kusu)

The island's two swimming lagoons are a popular destination for day-trippers. The warm fringing waters are ideal for swimming among hard and soft corals, pelagic fish, sea fans, sea snakes and turtles. Dolphins are sometimes seen as well.

Visit the charming Chinese Temple, Da Ba Gong (Temple of the Merchant God), which attracts 130,000 people on the ninth month of the lunar calendar, and the Malay shrine Kramat Kusu. And be sure to take in the stunning views of the mainland from the hilltop.

Southeast of Sentosa
Ferry from Marina South Pier. Departure times: Mon–Fri 10, 2, Sat 9, 12, 3, Sun 9, 11, 1, 3, 5
Return ticket S$18 adults, S$12 children 3 to 12 years
☎ 1800-736 8672 (freephone in Singapore)
Average Visibility: 3ft (1m)
Maximum Depth: 100ft (30m)

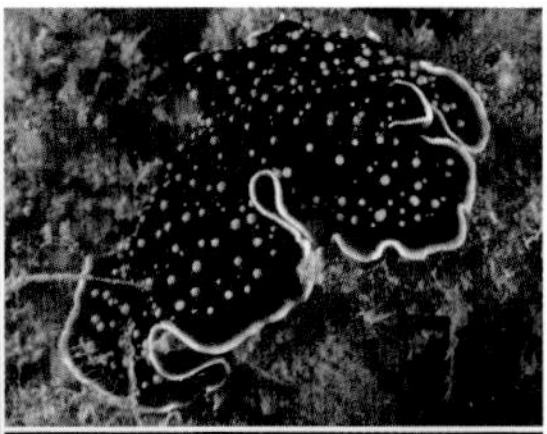

A six-banded angelfish (above) and a marine flatworm (above right)

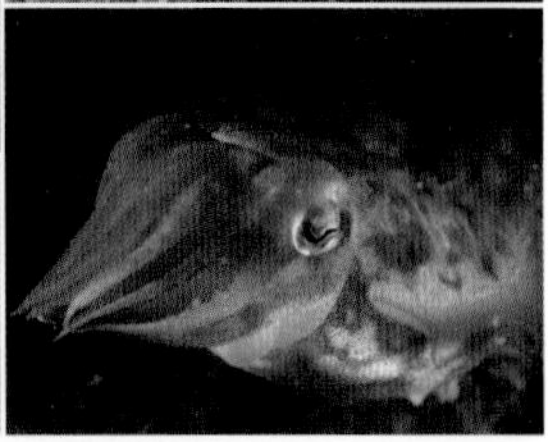

A squid

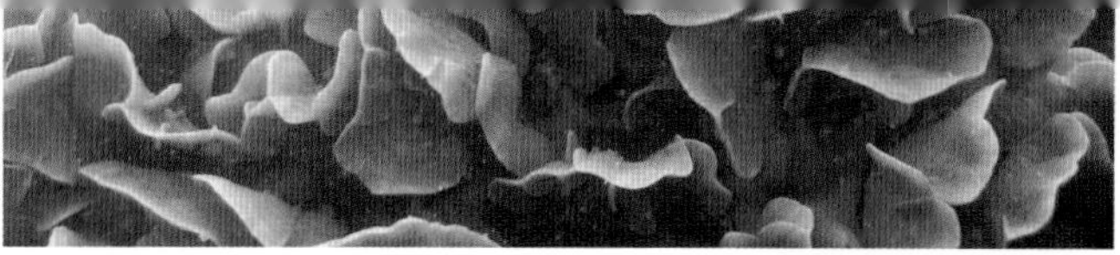

Lazarus Island and Sisters' Islands

These three tiny islands, just south of Singapore, have sandy beaches and are perfect for swimming, snorkeling and scuba diving. Since the currents are strong, divers should be experienced. On the southern tip of Lazarus Island there is a wreck at 60ft (18m). Sisters' Islands (Pulau Subar Laut and Pulau Subar Darat) are two little islands, which, legend has it, are two sisters who drowned while trying to escape from a pirate chief who wanted to marry one of them. Each island has shallow reefs and a bathing lagoon, but the current between the islands is swift and dangerous.

Lazarus Island

Between St. John's Island and Kusu Island
Causeway to St John's
Return ticket S$9 adults, S$6 children 3 to 12 years
1800-736 8672 (freephone in Singapore)
Average Visibility: 3ft (1m)
Maximum Depth: 60ft (18m)

Sisters' Islands

South of Sentosa
Must charter ferry from Marina South Pier
1800-736 8672 (freephone in Singapore)
Average Visibility: 5ft (1.5m)
Maximum Depth: 70ft (21m)

SURVIVING

Traveling to the islands and getting around them is hot, thirsty work and you need to understand how to prevent dehydration and how to notice if you have it. On a hot day, it may take as little as 15 minutes to become dehydrated and the following are signs: dry lips and tongue, apathy and lack of energy, muscle cramping, and bright-color or dark urine.

To prevent dehydration:
- Wear loose, light-color clothing
- Drink plenty of water
- Consume ample electrolytes (sodium and potassium dissolved in water)
- Cool off by pouring water over your head and neck

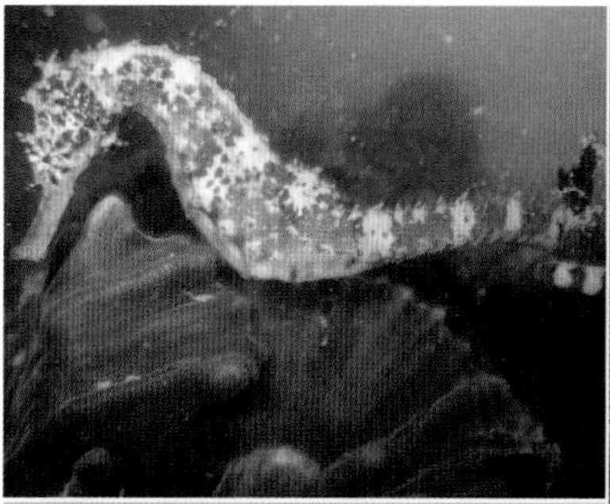

A tigertail seahorse

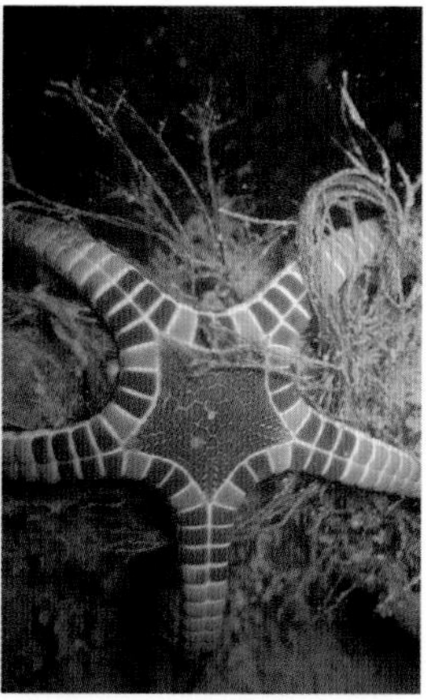

An icon seastar

Excursions

THE BASICS

www.brf.com.sg
Off map to southeast
Ferries leave Tanah Merah Ferry Terminal (6276 9722) several times a day—the trip takes about 45 min
Bintan Resort Ferries
6542 4369
Expensive

BINTAN

Bintan Island is about 28 miles (45km) southeast of Singapore, in the Riau Archipelago, the third largest province of Indonesia. An excellent excursion from Singapore, the island provides an introduction to Indonesian culture and, although the friendly locals speak Bahasa Indonesian, they enjoy practicing their English.

North and South Numerous seaside resorts, hotels and chalets, catering to a wide range of budgets, cover the northern shores of the island and are separated from the rest of the island by checkpoints and security guards. The southern part of the island is more populated and industrial, with electronics factories, fishing villages and bustling towns with thousands of motorcycles.

Island life Tanjung Pinang is the largest town on the island. The old, central market area, built on stilts, is a fascinating place and small enough to walk around. Try the delicious local fruit and seafood, and browse the interesting shops and markets. Pulau Penyengat, a 10-minute bumboat ride from Tanjung Pinang pier, has a charming fishing village, the remains of an old palace, and a mosque dating from 1880.

Practicalities Local time is one hour behind Singapore time. Bring cash in rupiah for use in the shops and at street stalls; Singapore dollars and credit cards are sometimes accepted for accommodations and food. Make sure you have your passport and check to see if you need a visa for entry. Most travelers can get a visa on arrival (VOA). Once you arrive, you fill in an arrival/departure card and pay US$25 for a 7-day stay.

JOHOR BAHRU

Johor Bahru is at the southern tip of the Malay Peninsula, just a short ride across the causeway from Singapore. Also referred to as JB, the state capital of Johor is a thriving commercial and administrative centre, with many shopping malls, hotels, restaurants and entertainment venues.

Choices Hotels in the city suit every taste and budget—there are resorts, international hotels and budget accommodations. Numerous night-clubs, discos, karaoke bars and cinemas can be found in the heart of the city and, after sunset, a sumptuous array of food stalls appear along the streets. There are also plenty of hawker centers and restaurants offering traditional Malay, Indian and Chinese delicacies.

Shopping and sightseeing The favorable exchange rate and tempting bargains in the big shopping malls, handicraft centers, bazaars and markets make JB a popular shopping destination with Singaporeans and overseas tourists. The Royal Sultan Abu Bakar Museum (Grand Palace) and its immaculate gardens, the beautiful Sultan Abu Bakar Mosque, and the Johor Art Gallery are some of JB's more famous historical and cultural attractions. The city is also a good point of departure for Malaysia's East Coast.

How to get there Take a Malaysian taxi from Rochor Road, where you can share a taxi, or book a specially licensed Singapore taxi. Buses run regularly from the Queen Street terminal in central Singapore. A ferry link operates daily between Changi Point near the Singapore International Airport and Tanjung Belungkor in Johor.

THE BASICS

b1
Malaysia Tourism Promotion Board:
www.tourism.gov.my
2 Jalan Ayer Molek, Johor Bahru 80000, Johor
607 222 3590 / 3591
Fax: 607 223 5502
Taxi: Johor Taxi Service
6296 7054

Royal Sultan Abu Bakar Museum
Jalan Tun Dr. Ismail, 15-min walk west of border
607 223 0555
Sat–Thu 9–4
Inexpensive

Pulau Ubin Sensory Trail

Pack sunblock and water, and head to the Sensory Trail, which displays Asian plants used for food, medicines and everyday items.

DISTANCE: 1 mile (1.5km) **ALLOW:** 60–90 min, best attempted early in the day

START

PULAU UBIN JETTY

e2 Tampines, then bus 29 to Changi Village. 10-min bumboat ride from Changi Jetty to the jetty at Pulau Ubin

1 Walk through the little village that surrounds the jetty to the visitors' center, just a short distance from the jetty, on the right. Ask at the center for a map of the walk.

2 The trail starts in the Spice and Herb Garden with a walk alongside a cool, shady banana grove. This useful plant is a good source of energy and vitamins and the leaves are used as food wrappers and disposable plates.

3 The pathway continues past a huge field of fragrant pandan. The scented leaves are often used in Asian cooking for coloring and flavoring. Next are plantings of the grass citronella, long leafstalks of torch ginger, curry trees, climbing beans, passion-fruit, guava, Aloe vera, the elephant yam, and finally a grove of sugarcane.

4 The trail goes on to the second section of the walk, which takes you through coastal forest and mangrove habitat. Here you'll see spiky pandanus (the leaves are used to make mats and baskets), mangrove trees, sea hibiscus (strings and cords are made from the bark), and betel nut palms (the nut is used in traditional Malay medicine).

5 Next you'll visit the island's coconut plantations, where you can take a break and buy a cold drink or try some fresh coconut milk, straight from the coconut.

6 Take the trail back to the center of the main village for a look around the shops, a fresh tropical fruit drink and a delicious seafood meal. Have a rest in the shade before you head back to the mainland.

END

PULAU UBIN JETTY

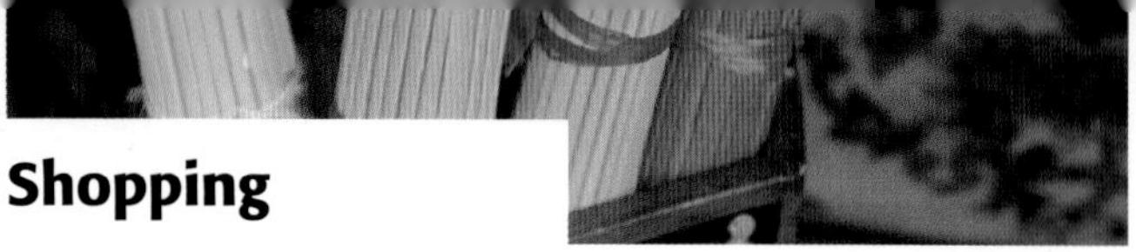

Shopping

BINTAN MALL

You'll find a variety of clothing, specialty and gift stores, and lots of stalls selling tasty Indonesian food at this bustling mall.
Off map to south
Jalan Pos, Tanjung Pinang, Bintan 62 7731 8041
Daily 10–10

JOHOR BAHRU DUTY FREE COMPLEX (ZON)

www.zon.com.my
The largest duty-free complex in Malaysia is packed with electronic goods, clothing, alcohol, chocolates and brand-name goods of all descriptions. Just 1.2 miles (2km) from the Singapore Causeway, ZON is easily accessible via daily international ferry services from Tanah Merah Ferry Terminal.
Off map to west
88 Jalan Ibrahim Sultan Stulang Laut, Johor Bahru
607227 4045
Daily 11–10 Regular buses from Customs area 6am–11pm

PLAZA PELANGI

A multitude of stores offer a wide array of value-for-money quality merchandise, from handicraft items and souvenirs to large selections of fashion apparel, accessories and trendy footwear. There are also eateries, a patisserie and fast-food outlets.
Off map to west 2 Jalan Kuning, Taman Pelangi, Johor Bahru 607 218 1818
Daily 10–10 Regular buses from Customs area 6am–11pm

Restaurants

PRICES

Prices are approximate, based on a 3-course meal for one person.

$$$	over S$50
$$	S$20–S$50
$	under S$20

BANYAN TREE BINTAN ($$$)

www.banyantree.com
The finest luxury beach resort this side of Bali has a wealth of restaurant options that are worth the trip to Bintan. There are three restaurants—Saffron, Treetops and The Cove—but the real attractions are the exclusive dining packages, which involve candlelit meals-for-two beside the South China Sea in the most private extremities of the resort.
Off map Jalan Teluk Berembang Laguna Bintan, Lagoi, Bintan, Indonesia
62 770 693 100 Daily 6.30am–10.30pm. Private dinners after 6pm every night

NEW HONG KONG RESTAURANT ($)

www.nhkrestaurant.com
A popular Cantonese restaurant, housed in two double-story shophouses with Oriental decor, specializes in dim sum and a variety of fish, poultry and vegetable dishes.
b1 69–A Jalan Ibrahim Sultan, Johor Bahru
607 222 2608 Mon–Sat 11–3, 6–10

SEASON "LIVE" SEAFOOD ($$)

Sit at makeshift tables, sip fresh coconut juice and enjoy a seafood lunch of steamed king prawns, tofu seafood soup, and crabs fried with spicy black pepper.
2e 59E Pulau Ubin, Singapore 6542 7627
Daily 12–2, 5–10

TAMAN SRI TEBRAU HAWKER CENTRE ($)

Around 50 stalls sell the best Malaysian fare to be found under one roof. Try Penang-fried *kuay teow,* satay or Hokkien prawn *mee.*
Off map to west Jalan Keris, Johor Bahru 607 218 1818 Daily 10–10

Where to Stay

In Singapore you'll find some of the world's best hotels, such as Raffles, while at lower prices, places such as YMCA International House offer comfortable and clean accommodation in a prime location.

Introduction

Singapore is a city that caters to the whole range of accommodation styles and price ranges. Choose from backpacker hostels and boutique hotels through to top-of-the-range five-star quality hotels such as the Mandarin Oriental or historic Raffles. All are very well equipped and offer standard room facilities as well as fitness centers and spas in the more exclusive places.

Business Options

For those who want to keep in touch with the business world while they are here, most hotels offer free WiFi services for guests. In many instances there are business facilities within the premises where remote meetings and conferences can take place. Whatever your needs and preferences, there will be a hotel here that fits your particular bill and purse.

Reservations

Be sure to make advance reservations to avoid having to compromise your budget by missing out on the low and mid-range accommodations, which are often fully booked. Of course, the internet is the way to go for bookings, and there are often seasonal specials on offer. And if you do arrive without prior reservations, the SHA hotel reservation counters at the airport will help you find a place to stay.

The STB's website (www.yoursingapore.com) also has a fantastic interactive booking service.

STAY AT THE AIRPORT

There are many reasons—delayed flight, lost booking, convenience—why you might like to stay at Singapore's international airport. Fortunately, all three terminals at Changi Airport have their own transit hotel, where for around S$60 per night you can rest in comfort, shower and change, swim in the pool, have a massage, or use the business center, all without the hassle of immigration and customs clearance, and without worrying about getting to the airport to catch your ongoing flight.

The range of accommodations options in Singapore is excellent

Budget Hotels

PRICES

Expect to pay under S$100 per person per night for a budget hotel.

BEN COOLEN
www.hotelbencoolen.com
This 84-room budget hotel is near the Singapore Art Museum and Little India and not far from Orchard Road and the Marina area.
F5 47 Bencoolen Street 6336 0822 Dhoby Ghaut, Bras Basah

BROADWAY
www.broadwayhotelsingapore.com
A Serangoon Road location puts this hotel in the middle of Little India. Standards are high and the staff friendly. Good Indian restaurant right next door.
F4 195 Serangoon Road 6292 4661; fax 6291 6414 Little India

FIVE STONES HOSTEL
www.fivestoneshostel.com
The nine rooms in this boutique hostel were all designed by local artists. The location is just a few steps away from Clarke Quay, but the hostel offers free ear plugs against late-night noise.
E6 61 South Bridge Road 6535 5607 Clarke Quay

MATCHBOX
www.matchbox.sg
Targeting hip backpackers headed to town, the three dormitory rooms are fitted with custom-made pods. Complimentary toiletries, daily breakfast and even free use of a massage chair are also provided for guests.
E7 39 Ann Siang Road 6423 0237 Chinatown

METROPOLITAN YMCA
www.mymca.org.sg
One of several YMCAs in Singapore, with a swimming pool. Book ahead.
C3 60 Stevens Road 6839 8333 MRT to Orchard then bus 196, 190, 132, 105, 605

PRINCE OF WALES
www.pow.com.sg
The Australian-run bar on the first floor is popular among expats, regularly hosting live music acts, with a backpacker hostel upstairs. The hostel offers free breakfast and lockers for guests.
F4 101 Dunlop Street 6299 0130 Little India

TRENDY HOSTELS

As the city was fast earning a reputation for having no budget accommodations, a few people took the initiative to open up inexpensive options with a bit of sass. Matchbox and Five Stones are both located in hip parts of town and offer low rates and unique amenities.

RELC INTERNATIONAL HOTEL
www.relcih.com.sg
Excellent value and location—Orchard Road is 10 minutes away. All rooms have a TV, a big bathroom, a fridge and a balcony.
C4 30 Orange Grove Road 6885 7888 Orchard

SLEEPY SAM'S BED & BREAKFAST
www.sleepysams.com
Coining itself as a "luxury hostel", this Kampong Glam hideaway offers both private bathrooms and dorms. There are tons of great stores and restaurants in the immediate vicinity.
G4 54 Bussorah Street 9277 4988 Bugis

STRAND
www.strandhotel.com.sg
A budget hotel with café and ensuite bathrooms.
F5 25 Bencoolen Street 6338 1866 Dhoby Ghaut

YMCA INTERNATIONAL HOUSE
www.ymcaih.com.sg
This YMCA, with a prime location near the start of Orchard Road, has a fitness facility and pool, and a McDonald's is in the building. Reserve well in advance.
E5 1 Orchard Road 6336 6000 Dhoby Ghaut

Mid-Range Hotels

PRICES

Expect to pay between S$100 and S$400 per person night for a mid-range hotel.

BERJAYA DUXTON HOTEL

www.berjayahotels-resorts.com

This classy hotel is a converted shophouse. Go for a duplex suite.

E8 83 Duxton Road 6227 7678 Tanjong Pagar

THE CLUB

www.theclub.com.sg

Occupying an old heritage building on hip Ann Siang Road, the 22-room boutique hotel is decorated in black and white. The rooftop lounge and basement whiskey bar are popular hangouts.

E7 28 Ann Siang Road 6808 2188 Chinatown

THE ELIZABETH SINGAPORE

www.theelizabeth.com

This small, comfortable hotel has a three-story-high series of waterfalls. Excellent value and good location. Restaurant, small outdoor pool and fitness area, 24-hour room service and babysitting.

D4 24 Mount Elizabeth 6738 1188 Orchard

FURAMA HOTEL SINGAPORE

www.furama.com/citycentre

In a great location in Chinatown, near Boat Quay and Clarke Quay, where there's plenty of shopping, dining and nightlife. Outdoor pool, two restaurants and fitness and business facilities.

E7 60 Eu Tong Sen Street 6533 3888 Chinatown

HOTEL 1929

www.hotel1929.com

The 32-room boutique hotel was hotelier and restaurateur Loh Lik Peng's first contribution to the city. The rooms are small but the funky artwork and prime Chinatown location make it a great pick.

E7 50 Keong Saik Road 6347 1929 Chinatown

HOTEL CLOVER

www.hotelclover.com

Ranging from windowless single rooms to suites with outdoor Jacuzzis, all the rooms sport a modern rustic design. The Kampong Glam location gives access to funky hookah lounges and trendy boutiques.

G4 769 North Bridge Road 6340 1860 Bugis

LOCATION

Singapore's mid-range hotels are scattered throughout the city center, and it is worth trying to find a hotel that suits your sightseeing tastes as much as your budget. Shoppers could consider the many Orchard Road and surrounds options, while lovers of Chinese art and culture may find that staying in Chinatown provides plenty of opportunity to seek out architectural and cultural aspects of Singapore that are fast disappearing.

HOTEL WINDSOR

www.hotelwindsor.com.sg

Good value for the money and easy access to the East Coast make this a popular choice. The Café Windsor serves continental cuisine and tasty local fare.

K1 401 Macpherson Road 6343 0088 Aljunied

INN AT TEMPLE STREET

www.theinn.com.sg

Right in the heart of Chinatown, this charming hotel has traditional Peranakan furniture in the lobby and guest rooms. Its café serves Western and Asian dishes.

E7 36 Temple Street 6221 5333 Chinatown 84, 166, 197

NAUMI LIORA

www.naumiliora.com

In an effort to pay tribute to the Peranakan-styled townhouses' heritage, designers of this Chinatown hotel left details like the original timber flooring and French-styled windows intact. Hip coffee joints and trendy bars line the surrounding streets.

E7 55 Keong Saik Road 6922 9000 Chinatown

PARKROYAL ON PICKERING

www.parkroyalhotels.com

Eco-friendly initiatives have been made throughout this Chinatown hotel. Spend an afternoon relaxing in the poolside cabanas or indulge in a treatment from the spa.

E7 3 Upper Pickering Street 6809 8888 Chinatown

PENINSULA EXCELSIOR

www.ytchotels.com.sg

Top value for money. An excellent location in the Historic District and you can walk to Chinatown from here. Restaurant and bar, two outdoor pools and babysitting.

F6 5 Coleman Street 6337 2200 City Hall

THE QUINCY

www.quincy.com.sg

The all-inclusive boutique hotel offers guests all meals and complimentary cocktails during happy hour. Just off the Orchard Road shopping belt, additional perks include a 24-hour pool and gym.

C4 22 Mount Elizabeth 6738 5888 Orchard

SWISSÔTEL MERCHANT COURT HOTEL

www.swissotel.com

This hotel, on the Singapore River between Clarke Quay and Chinatown, is always a good choice. The extensive facilities include a great pool, a business center, self-service laundry facilities and a relaxing lobby bar.

E6 20 Merchant Road 6337 2288 Clarke Quay

TRADERS HOTEL

This is near the Botanic Gardens and Orchard Road. Family apartments have small kitchens and rooms with foldaway beds.

C4 1A Cuscaden Road 6738 2222; fax 6831 4314 Orchard

VILLAGE HOTEL ALBERT COURT

www.albertcourt.com.sg

An eight-floor hotel comprising 210 rooms in a renovated shophouse near Little India, with café and good facilities.

F5 180 Albert Street 6339 3939 Bugis

TRAVEL TO YOUR HOTEL

Besides Singapore's modern and efficient public transportation system, taxis are everywhere and very affordable. Another convenient way to travel to and from Singapore's Changi Airport is to take a six-seater MaxiCab shuttle service, which operates daily from 6am to midnight. The service stops at Concorde Hotel Singapore, Peninsula Excelsior and Marina Mandarin Singapore, and has a flexible routing system between the airport and hotels within the city.

WANDERLUST

www.wanderlusthotel.com

Tucked away in a former schoolhouse in Little India, several local design agencies were given full creative freedom, emphatically expressed in the outrageous themes carried out in all 29 rooms of this boutique hotel.

E4 2 Dickson Road 6396 3322 Little India

WANGZ

www.wangzhotel.com

The tall cylindrical shape of this boutique hotel makes it stand out along the streets of the trendy Tiong Bahru neighbourhood. Guests can enjoy dining discounts at the rooftop bar and restaurant Halo.

C7 231 Outram Road 6595 1388 Tiong Bahru

YORK HOTEL SINGAPORE

www.yorkhotel.com.sg

A small hotel with spacious rooms, just a short walk away from Orchard Road. The restaurant, outdoor pool and sun deck with huge palms, 24-room service and babysitting are added attractions.

D4 21 Mount Elizabeth 6737 0511 Orchard

Luxury Hotels

PRICES

Expect to pay over S$400 per person per night for a luxury hotel.

FOUR SEASONS

www.fourseasons.com/singapore

Ideally located just behind Orchard Road, with top-notch facilities, two pools, air-conditioned tennis courts and good restaurants.

C4 190 Orchard Boulevard 6734 1110 Orchard

FULLERTON

www.fullertonhotel.com

Located in the heritage GPO building, the Fullerton has lovely river views.

F7 1 Fullerton Square 6735 8388 Raffles Place

GOODWOOD PARK

www.goodwood parkhotel.com.sg

Formerly the Teutonia Club for German expatriates, this hotel retains its charm. It is well located, close to Orchard Road, and has lovely gardens.

C4 22 Scotts Road 6737 7411 Orchard

MANDARIN ORIENTAL

www.mandarin-oriental.com/singapore

The 21-floor Mandarin Oriental is one of the hotels built on reclaimed land overlooking Marina Bay. It is close to Marina Square shopping mall—good for last-minute gifts—and Suntec City, which incorporates one of the largest conference and exhibition halls in Asia.

F6 5 Raffles Avenue, Marina Square 6339 8811 City Hall

MARINA MANDARIN

With a superb waterfront location in the Marina Bay, this 575-room luxury hotel offers the ultimate in facilities, including a host of recreation possibilities.

F6 6 Raffles Boulevard 6845 1000; fax 6845 1199 City Hall

MARRIOTT

www.marriott.com

This Singapore landmark, formerly the Dynasty, retains its original distinctive pagoda-style roof and features a roof-top pool and business and fitness facilities. Central location above Tangs store.

C4 320 Orchard Road 6735 8967 Orchard

CITY ICON

Marina Bay Sands' three-tower structure has become an iconic point on the city's skyline. Rooms offer views of the surrounding architecture or South China Sea and guests have the privilege of soaking in the rooftop infinity pool.

G7 10 Bayfront Avenue 6688 8868 Bayfront

RAFFLES

www.raffles.com

To relive the golden age of travel, stay at Raffles (▷ 38), Singapore's most famous hotel, first opened in 1887. All the accommodations are suites and are expensive.

F5 1 Beach Road 6337 1886 City Hall

RITZ-CARLTON MILLENIA

www.ritzcarlton.com

Ideal for business travelers and for visitors who can afford to splurge. A commanding position on Marina Bay provides fantastic views over the harbor and the Esplanade theater complex.

F6 7 Raffles Avenue 6337 8888 City Hall

SHANGRI-LA

www.shangri-la.com

One of Singapore's finest hotels, with all the facilities you'd expect, plus magnificent gardens and a golf putting green.

B3 22 Orange Grove Road 6737 3644 Orchard

SWISSÔTEL THE STAMFORD

www.swissotel.com

This luxury hotel has every possible amenity, including 16 restaurants, a business center, sports facilities and views.

F6 2 Stamford Road 6338 8585 City Hall

Need to Know

The more you plan your trip, the more you'll get out of your time in Singapore. Try to catch Chinese New Year (January/February), Chingay Parade (February), or the Great Singapore Sale (July).

Planning Ahead

When to Go

The best time to visit Singapore is around Chinese New Year, although you will need to book a hotel well in advance. July is sale time in Orchard Road, so shoppers take note. Otherwise, the city hums along year-round, catering to holiday and business travelers alike.

TIME

Singapore is 8 hours ahead of GMT, 13 hours ahead of New York, and 2 hours behind Sydney

AVERAGE DAILY MAXIMUM TEMPERATURES

JAN	FEB	MAR	APR	MAY	JUN	JUL	AUG	SEP	OCT	NOV	DEC
86°F	88°F	88°F	89°F	90°F	90°F	87°F	88°F	88°F	88°F	88°F	86°F
30°C	31°C	31°C	32°C	32°C	32°C	31°C	31°C	31°C	31°C	31°C	30°C

Weather Singapore's climate is tropical, with very few seasonal variations. The temperature range is steady, from a nighttime low of 75°F (24°C) to a daily high of 88°F (31°C). December and January can be slightly cooler and May to August slightly hotter. Rainfall peaks between November and January, with the northeast monsoon. However, it rarely rains for long—usually an hour's torrential downpour at a time. During monsoon times, storms can be dramatic, with sheets of rain and intense thunder and lightning. Most occur early in the morning and in the afternoon. Humidity can sometimes reach nearly 100 percent, and averages 84 percent.

WHAT'S ON

January *Art Stage Singapore:* Art from around the region is put in the global spotlight.
Thaipusam: This Hindu festival displays dramatic feats of mind over matter.
January/February *Chinese New Year:* A two-day public holiday, with fireworks, stalls and dragon dances.
February *Chingay Parade:* Huge street carnival based on a Chinese folk festival. Lion dancers, acrobats and floats.
March *Singapore Food Festival.*
April *Singapore International Film Festival*
June *Dragon Boat Festival:* 20 teams enter this colorful longboat race.
Singapore Arts Festival: One of Asia's leading contemporary arts festivals.
July *Great Singapore Sale:* Orchard Road hosts this price-cutting month around July, to highlight Singapore as a major shopping destination.
August *National Day:* 9 August. This public holiday marks Singapore's independence from the British.
August/September *Festival of the Hungry Ghosts:* Fun and feasting.
September *Mooncake Festival:* A colorful spectacle named after the delicious mooncakes on sale.
Singapore Grand Prix: Formula 1's only night race, held in Marina Bay.
October *Thimithi:* Fire-walking ceremony.
October/November *Festival of the Nine Emperor Gods:* A week of processions and street opera.
November *Deepavali:* Lamps are lit to celebrate the triumph of good over evil.
December *Christmas:* Orchard Road lights up.

Singapore Online

Not surprisingly, Singapore has been fully wired for broadband and has embraced the global digital culture.

www.yoursingapore.com
This dynamic site, written in 10 languages, is the official Singapore Tourism website and has up-to-date details of events, exhibitions, holiday ideas and shopping, dining and accommodations suggestions.

www.asia1.com.sg
Singapore's main media group's portal. Links to all major national print media websites, plus international and regional news.

www.singapore.tourism-asia.net
Plenty of up-to-date information on this site, with good sections on general travel, attractions, shopping and entertainment.

www.asiatravelmart.com
Asia's major online travel marketplace with various hotel and flight booking information, plus booking online.

www.nhb.gov.sg/MCC
Visitor information for the Asian Civilisations Museum, the Singapore Art Museum and a World War II museum at Bukit Chandu—comprehensive descriptions, photos and locations.

www.insing.com
Restaurant reviews, local gossip and shopping tips—and restaurant reservations can be made here as well.

www.singaporeforkids.com
This website gives a light-hearted insight into unusual things to do in Singapore that will be fun for both kids and adults.

GOOD TRAVEL SITES

www.fodors.com
A complete travel-planning site. You can research prices and weather; book air tickets, cars and rooms; ask questions (and get answers) from fellow travelers; and find links to other sites.

www.changiairport.com
Features arrival and departure details, airport facilities, and shopping and dining information in all terminals.

INTERNET ACCESS

All hotels offer internet access; some provide free WiFi.
Wireless@SG is a scheme that provides free wireless connection at selected hotspots. You will need a mobile device with WiFi facility, such as smartphone, laptop or tablet, and you have to register online with a service provider: iCELL (www.icellnetwork.com), M1 (www.m1net.com.sg) or SingTel (www.singtel.com). For the latest on Wireless@SG's coverage, see the IDA's website, www.ida.gov.sg.

Getting There

INFORMATION

For airport inquiries ☎ 6595 6868; www.changiairport.com.sg.

CAR RENTAL

- Car rental is expensive and public transportation is very good.
- An electronic road pricing system is installed in all cars, requiring rental drivers to pay Central Business District crossing line fees (during peak hours only).
- Display coupons in your windscreen in parking lots and designated parking places. Area day licenses and books of coupons can be purchased at newsagents, 7-Eleven and garages. Steep fines are incurred for failing to display licenses and coupons.
- Driving is on the left. A valid international or other recognized driver's license is required.
- Insurance is included in most rental fees.

AIRPORTS

Singapore's Changi Airport is 12 miles (20km) east of the city center. Flights take around 13 hours from Western Europe and around 20 hours from the US. The huge airport has several terminals, many lounges and hundreds of shops.

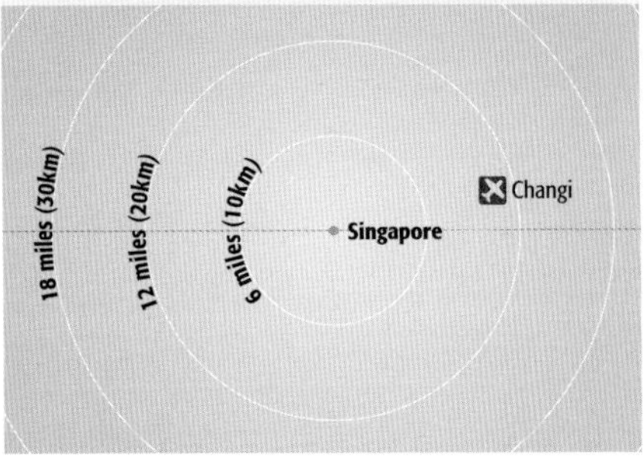

FROM CHANGI AIRPORT

Take the MRT train connection for easy access to all parts of the island. You can go to Tanah Merah station and switch to the westbound train service to be in the city in less than 30 minutes; the fare is less than S$2
Inquiries ☎ 1800 336 8900.
Taxi ranks are well marked and the lines always move quickly. The fare into the city is around S$25.

The airport shuttle service (☎ 6543 1985) stops at major hotels in the city (journey time 30 minutes; cost S$9). It runs 24 hours and can be picked up from just outside the terminal.

Public bus 36 travels to the city (6am to midnight, journey time 50 minutes; cost S$2). Pick it up below terminals 1, 2 and 3.

Car rental counters can be found in the Arrivals Hall of all three terminals and operate between 7am and 11pm.

ARRIVING BY BUS

Air-conditioned long-distance buses come direct from Bangkok, Penang and Kuala Lumpur, as well as from other main towns on the Malaysian Peninsula. To help make sense

of the many services operating routes between Malaysia and Singapore, visit Easibook (www.easibook.com), an online resource to compare fees and to locate the most convenient ticketing office and departure location. Buses between Singapore and Kuala Lumpur take around 6 hours, with prices starting at S$28. A bus ride to Bangkok takes around 28 hours, with fares starting at S$85.

Another website providing bus service information to and from Singapore is www.myexpressbus.com, covering companies that include Aeroline, Five Stars Travel, Grassland Express and Konsortium Express.

Odyssey (www.odysseynow.com.my), a more recent luxury addition to the Singapore–Kuala Lumpur bus service, boasts leather recliners, wide leg room, a personal TV and meals along the way. Prices start at around S$40 each way.

Long-distance buses from Malaysia arrive and depart from the Lavender Street bus station.

Bus 170 leaves the bus station at Johor Bahru (the Malaysian city visible across the causeway from Singapore) regularly for Ban San bus station in Singapore (Singapore–Johor Bahru Express ☎ 6292 8149; journey time 1 hour; cost S$1.90). The Second Crossing, another causeway, links Tuas in Singapore's west with Malaysia's Johor state. All bus travelers break their journeys for immigration formalities.

ARRIVING BY SEA

Most cruise ships dock at the Marina Bay Cruise Centre. From there, taxis and buses go to central Singapore. Ferries travel regularly between Tanjong Belungkor (Johor) and Changi ferry terminal (Ferrylink ☎ 6545 3600; journey time 45 minutes; cost S$25); to and from Tioman March to October (Auto Batam Ferries ☎ 6271 4866; journey time 4 hours 30 minutes; cost S$120); and between HarbourFront and Bintan (Auto Batam Ferries ☎ 6271 4866; journey time 1 hour 30 minutes; cost S$50).

VACCINATIONS

Vaccinations are unnecessary unless you are coming from an area infected with yellow fever or cholera.

ENTRY REQUIREMENTS

Visas are not required by citizens of the EU, US or most Commonwealth countries (although Indian visitors staying more than 4 days require a visa). Passports must be valid for at least 6 months. On arrival, tourist visas are issued for 30 days. Extensions are available from the Immigration and Checkpoints Authority ☎ 6391 6100 (10 Kallang Road) www.app.lca.gov.sg or by making a trip outside Singapore. Passport and visa regulations can change at short notice, so always check before you travel.

AIRPORT HOTEL

Terminals 1, 2 and 3 have 73 transit hotel rooms each. Rentals are from S$77 per 6-hour block for single occupancy.

Getting Around

TOURIST BOARD

● Singapore Tourism produces lots of printed material about the island's attractions and tours and there are any number of brochures available from hotel reception desks. But the Touristline is handy for after-hours information and visitor centers are always worth a visit.

Touristline: ☎ 1800 736 2000 (toll-free in Singapore). (65) 6736 2000 (overseas).
Chinatown: ✉ 2 Banda Street (behind Buddha Tooth Relic Temple) 🕐 Mon–Fri 9–9, Sat–Sun 9am–10pm 🚇 Chinatown

Orchard: ✉ Junction of Cairnhill Road and Orchard Road 🕐 9.30am to 10.30pm daily 🚇 Somerset
● Overseas tourist offices: Australia Level 11, AWA Building, 47 York Street, Sydney, NSW 2000 ☎ 02 9290 2882/8; fax 02 9290 2555
UK ✉ Grand Buildings, 1–3 Strand, London WC2N 5HR ☎ 020 7484 2710
US ✉ 1156 Avenue of the Americas, Suite 702, New York, NY 10036 ☎ 212/302 4861; fax 212/302 4801

BUSES

● Buses take exact change, though you can always give a dollar coin for a journey you know costs less.
● Buses are numerous and frequent. Buy individual tickets on the bus (exact change only), or use the ez-link card.
● Machines at the front of the bus take the card; press a button for the price of your particular journey. If you're not sure of the amount, ask the driver.
● A comprehensive bus and MRT timetable, called the Transitlink Guide, can be purchased at newsagents for S$1.50.
● Singapore Bus Service runs a hotline 🕐 Mon–Fri 8–5.30, Sat 8–1. Tell them where you are and where you want to go. The number is ☎ 1800 336 8900.
● SMRT Buses also operate a night service, called the NightRider, offering late or early morning travelers a safe and affordable means of travel. The fare for this service is S$3 per trip regardless of whether you are paying by cash or ez-link card. Concessionary travel is not available for this service.

MRT

● There are four main mass rapid transit (MRT) lines; north–south, east–west, north–east and circle. Downtown line is currently under construction.
● Trains run between 5.30am and 12.30am.
● You can buy single tickets, or use the S$7 tourist souvenir stored-value cards for a number of journeys.
● The ez-link card, also a stored-value card (minimum value S$10 plus S$5 deposit), can be used on buses as well as the MRT.
● Cards can be purchased from machines and from ticket offices. Tap them on machines at the barriers when entering and leaving stations.
● At the end of your stay refunds can be obtained on any amount outstanding on stored-value cards.

- Useful numbers:
- MRT ☎ 1800 767 4333; MRT and bus integration ☎ 1800 336 8900

TAXIS

- Taxis are easily found on Singapore's roads, though they can be more difficult to come by during rush hours (8am–9am and 5pm–7pm), just before midnight, and when it's raining.
- Shopping centers, hotels, sights and stations usually have taxi stands, and apart from these, taxis can also be hailed along the road. A taxi displaying a light at night is for hire.
- Taxis are air-conditioned and comfortable.
- Taxis charge a surcharge of S$3–S$5. There are surcharges for taxis hired from the airport, for fares between midnight and 6am, for bookings made in advance, for rush hours and for journeys via the business district or on roads where electronic road-pricing schemes are operating.
- Taxi drivers sometimes may not have sufficient change to accept large notes (S$50 or higher), so carry some low-value notes.
- Reserve in advance for important journeys, such as to the airport. Some taxi companies:
Comfort ☎ 6552 1111
Citycab ☎ 6552 2222
Comfort Premier Cabs ☎ 6552 2828
- Watch out for the Chrysler taxis, as the fare starts higher and also increases more rapidly.

TRISHAWS

- Singapore's trishaws are now confined to a few inner-city locations where they can be hired for a ride back in time. Tour operators will also organize group tours to the back streets of Chinatown and Little India. Trishaw rides last an average of 30–45 minutes and cost from S$50 per person.
- Tour around Chinatown: Trishaw Uncle (www.trishawuncle.com.sg) offers tours around the city.

NEIGHBORHOODS

- Singapore's near-city neighborhoods—each one with a distinct character—are within easy reach by bus or MRT (Mass Rapid Transit). South of the river, Chinatown comes alive at festival time and just to the north is the CBD, with its tall office towers; across the river, the colonial district is set around the Padang, several museums and Raffles Hotel. Heading westward, busy Orchard Road is an international retail hub and along Serangoon Road, to the north, Indian culture thrives. Nearby Kampong Glam has long been at the heart of Malay culture. But try to discover some more out-of-the-way places, such as delightful Pulau Ubin, off the northeast of the island, or any one of the masses of public housing precincts where Singaporeans live.

VISITORS WITH DISABILITIES

Many hotels, shops and sights have facilities for people with disabilities, though getting around can sometimes be difficult because the MRT and buses are not wheelchair friendly.
If you have specific queries about particular problems, contact the National Council of Social Services ☎ 6336 1544.

Essential Facts

INSURANCE

Check your insurance policy and purchase supplementary coverage if necessary. Make sure you are covered for medical expenses.

MONEY

The unit of currency is the Singapore dollar. Brunei dollar notes have the same value as the Singapore dollar and are often accepted in Singapore. The Singapore dollar and other major currencies are easily changed to local currency in Malaysia and Indonesia. Traveler's checks are readily accepted.

MAGAZINES AND NEWSPAPERS

- The main English-language dailies are the *Straits Times*, the *Business Times*, *Today* and the *New Paper*. The latter is of a tabloid nature, seen as a fun alternative to others and as a result contains very little real news.
- The *International New York Times* is also available, as is a wide range of local and international magazines and publications.
- *Time Out Singapore*, *I-S* magazine and *Juice* are all good for listings.

MAIL

- Post office hours vary, but the post office at 1 Killiney Road is open Mon–Sat 9–9, Sun 9–4.30.
- Buy stamps in small shops and hotel lobbies, as well as at post offices.
- Postcards and airmail letters to all destinations cost 50 cents. Standard letter rate to Europe/US is S$1. Prepaid postcards and airmail letters are available.

MEDICAL TREATMENT

- Singapore's medical system is world-class. It offers a mixture of public and private treatment options. Make sure you have insurance cover.
- Many hotels offer guests a doctor-on-call service or can recommend a local doctor or clinic for you.
- If you require hospital treatment, you will need to provide proof that you can pay for it.
- The best centrally located hospitals are Mount Elizabeth (☎ 6737 2666) and Gleneagles (☎ 6473 7222). Both have emergency departments.
- Most medicines are available in Singapore.

MONEY MATTERS

- You can change money at the airport on arrival, or at hotels, banks and moneychangers, who can be found all over town (and whose rate is slightly better than that given by banks and hotels). Most major banks are in the

Central Business District (CBD).
- ATMs are everywhere.
- Many shops, restaurants and hotels take credit cards.

OPENING HOURS
- Stores: usually Mon–Sat 10–9.30; some close earlier and others keep longer hours. Most shops are open on Sunday.
- Banks: Mon–Fri 9–3, Sat 10–12.
- Offices: usually Mon–Fri 9–5; some open for half a day on Saturday and others open earlier and close later.
- Doctors' clinics: Mon–Fri 9–6, Sat 9–noon.

PUBLIC HOLIDAYS
- New Year's Day: 1 January
- Hari Raya Puasa: one day, January/February
- Chinese New Year: two days, January/February
- Good Friday: March/April
- Hari Raya Haji: one day, April
- Labour Day: 1 May
- Vesak Day: one day, May
- National Day: 9 August
- Deepavali: October/November
- Christmas Day: 25 December

TELEPHONES
- Phone calls within Singapore are very cheap—local calls cost as little as 10 cents for three-minute blocks.
- Phone cards for public phones (increasingly rare nowadays) can be purchased at stores and post offices.
- Calls from some hotels are subject to a 20 percent surcharge.
- International calls need to be prefixed by 001, followed by the country code. To call Singapore from outside, use country code 65.
- Operator to call for Singapore numbers ☎ 100; international numbers ☎ 104

EMBASSIES AND CONSULATES
- Australia ✉ 25 Napier Road ☎ 6836 4100 🕐 Mon–Fri 8.30–12.30 and 1.30–5
- Canada ✉ 1 George Street, 11-01 ☎ 6854 5900 🕐 Mon–Thu 8–12.30, 1–4.30, Fri 8–12.30
- India ✉ 31 Grange Road ☎ 6737 6777 🕐 Mon–Fri 9–1, 1.30–5.30
- Indonesia ✉ 7 Chatsworth Road ☎ 6737 7422 🕐 Mon–Fri 9–5
- Ireland ✉ 541 Orchard Road, 08-00 Liat Towers ☎ 6238 7616 🕐 9.30–12.30, 2–5
- Malaysia ✉ 301 Jervois Road ☎ 6235 0111 🕐 Mon–Fri 8–5.15
- New Zealand ✉ 391A Orchard Road, 15-06 Ngee Ann City Tower A ☎ 6738 6700 🕐 Mon–Fri 9.30–4
- UK ✉ 100 Tanglin Road ☎ 6424 4200 🕐 Mon–Fri 8.30–5
- US ✉ 27 Napier Road ☎ 6476 9100 🕐 Mon–Fri 8.30–5.15

LOST PROPERTY
- Police ☎ 999
- For lost credit cards:
American Express ☎ 1800 737 8188;
Diners Card ☎ 6294 4222;
MasterCard ☎ 1800 110 0113;
VISA ☎ 1800 110 0344

Language

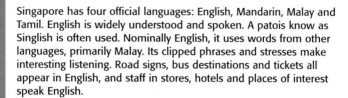

Singapore has four official languages: English, Mandarin, Malay and Tamil. English is widely understood and spoken. A patois know as Singlish is often used. Nominally English, it uses words from other languages, primarily Malay. Its clipped phrases and stresses make interesting listening. Road signs, bus destinations and tickets all appear in English, and staff in stores, hotels and places of interest speak English.

USEFUL WORDS AND PHRASES

MALAY	ENGLISH
selamat pagi	good morning
selamat petang	good afternoon
selamat malam	goodnight
selamat tinggal, selamat jalan	good-bye
api khabar?	how are you?
khabar baik	I'm fine
ya	yes
tidak	no
tidak apa	never mind
terimah kasih	thank you
sama sama	you're welcome
baiklah	OK
bila?	when?
esok	tomorrow
hari ini	today
semalam	yesterday
berapa har ganya?	how much?
mahal	expensive
murah	cheap
berapa jauh?	how far?
di mana?	where?

FOOD AND DRINK

daging lembu	beef
ayam	chicken
ikan	fish
daging babi	pork
nasi	rice
nasi goreng	fried rice
mee goreng	fried noodles
sayur	vegetables
kopi	coffee
teh	tea

NUMBERS

satu	1
dua	2
tiga	3
empat	4
lima	5
sitta	6
tujuh	7
lapan	8
sembilan	9
sepuluh	10
sebelas	11
dua belas	12
tifa belas	13
dua puluh	20
tiga puluh	30
empat puluh	40
lima puluh	50
seratus	100
seribu	1,000

DAYS

senin, isnin	Monday
selasa	Tuesday
rabu	Wednesday
khamis	Thursday
jumaat	Friday
sabtu	Saturday
ahad	Sunday

Timeline

EARLY DAYS

The first mention of Singapore comes in Chinese seafaring records of the 3rd century AD, where it is referred to as "Pu lou Chung" (island at the end of the peninsula). In the late 13th century Marco Polo noted a thriving city, possibly a satellite of the flourishing Sumatran Srivijayan empire. It could have been Singapore, then called Temasek. Sejarah Melayu (Malay annals of the 16th century) note a 13th-century Singapura (Lion City).
In the late 14th century, the island's ruler, Parameswara, fled to Melaka. For 400 years Singapore was all but abandoned except for visiting pirates and fishermen.

1819 British official Thomas Stamford Raffles selects Singapore as a trading post between China and India. It is also near to newly acquired British colonies.

1826 With Penang and Melaka, Singapore becomes part of the British-run Straits Settlements.

1867 Singapore is designated a Crown Colony under British rule. It becomes a hub of international trade.

1870s Thousands of immigrants from south China begin arriving in Singapore. They work in shipyards and rubber plantations, and as small traders.

1887 Henry Ridley, director of the Botanic Gardens, propagates Asia's first rubber trees. Raffles Hotel opens.

1921 Japan's increasing military might causes the British to start building coastal defenses.

1942 Singapore falls to the Japanese.

1945 British Lord Louis Mountbatten accepts the Japanese surrender.

1954 Singapore's first elections: a legislative council is elected to advise the governor. Lee Kuan Yew helps found the People's Action Party (PAP).

Left to right: Sir Stamford Raffles, founder of Singapore; Raffles Hotel; plaque at Old Ford Factory; Chinatown temple detail; an old newspaper at Old Ford Factory; artwork at a Chinatown temple

1955 A Legislative Assembly is set up. David Marshall becomes Singapore's first chief minister.

1957 Malaya becomes independent. Singapore is a separate colony.

1959 PAP forms Singapore's first government. Lee Kuan Yew is appointed prime minister.

1963 Singapore forms the Federation of Malaysia together with Malaya, Sarawak and North Borneo.

1965 Singapore leaves the Federation and becomes an independent republic.

1966 The Singapore dollar becomes the official currency.

1968 The British announce military withdrawl. First parliamentary general election.

1977 2,913 acres (1,179 hectares) of land is reclaimed from the sea.

1990 Lee Kuan Yew steps aside, into the newly created post of senior minister.

2000 Singapore recovers from the Asian economic crisis.

2011 First presidential election, won by Tony Tan.

JAPANESE OCCUPATION

In 1942 the Japanese launched their attack on Singapore. Despite being outnumbered three to one, they gained control of the colony in just a few days, during which time tens of thousands of British, Indian and Australian troops were killed or wounded. During the occupation up to 50,000 Chinese men were executed and the Allied troops were interned or dispatched to work on the infamous "Death" railway.

LEE KUAN YEW

Lee Kuan Yew is credited with transforming Singapore from a Third World trading port to a highly developed nation. Known for hard work and discipline, he encouraged developments in housing, education, infrastructure and manufacture, with amazing results.

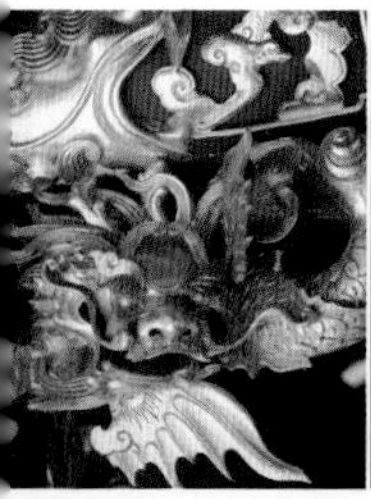

Index

Singapore 25 Best

WRITTEN BY Vivien Lytton
ADDITIONAL WRITING Rod Ritchie
UPDATED BY Alexandra Karplus
SERIES EDITOR Clare Ashton
COVER DESIGN Chie Ushio, Yuko Inagaki
DESIGN WORK Tracey Freestone
IMAGE RETOUCHING AND REPRO Ian Little

Published in the United Kingdom by AA Publishing

ISBN 978-0-8041-4349-3

FIFTH EDITION

All details in this book are based on information supplied to us at press time. Always confirm information when it matters, especially if you're making a detour to visit a specific place. Fodor's expressly disclaims any liability, loss, or risk, personal or otherwise, that is incurred as a consequence of the use of any of the contents of this book.

SPECIAL SALES
This book is available for special discounts for bulk purchases for sales promotions or premiums. For more information, email specialmarkets@randomhouse.com.

Color separation by AA Digital Department
Printed and bound by Leo Paper Products, China

10 9 8 7 6 5 4 3 2 1

A05141
Maps in this title produced from mapping © MAIRDUMONT / Falk Verlag 2013 and from data from openstreetmap.org © Open Street Map contributors
Transport map © Communicarta Ltd, UK

The Automobile Association would like to thank the following photographers, companies and picture libraries for their assistance in the preparation of this book.

Abbreviations for the picture credits are as follows: - (t) top; (b) bottom; (l) left; (r) right; (c) center; (AA) AA World Travel Library.

1 AA/N Setchfield; **2–18t** Courtesy of Singapore Tourism Board; **4tl** AA/N Setchfield; **5** AA/N Setchfield; **6cl** AA/N Setchfield; **6c** AA/N Setchfield; **6cr** Courtesy of Singapore Tourism Board; **6bl** AA/N Setchfield; **6bc** Courtesy of Singapore Tourism Board; **6br** Courtesy of Singapore Tourism Board; **7cl** Courtesy of Media Bank; **7c** AA/N Setchfield; **7cr** Courtesy of Singapore Tourism Board; **7bl** Courtesy of Singapore Tourism Board; **7br** Brand X Pics; **10tr** Courtesy of Singapore Tourism Board; **10tcr** AA/N Setchfield; **10/11c** AA/N Setchfield; **10/11b** AA/N Setchfield; **11tl** AA/N Setchfield; **11tcl** Courtesy of Singapore Tourism Board; **12** Courtesy of Singapore Tourism Board; **13(i)** Courtesy of Singapore Tourism Board; **13(ii)** Courtesy of Singapore Tourism Board; **13(iii)** AA/N Setchfield; **13(iv)** Courtesy of Singapore Tourism Board; **13(v)** Courtesy of Singapore Tourism Board; **14tr** AA/N Setchfield; **14tcr** AA/N Setchfield; **14cr** AA/N Setchfield; **14br** Courtesy of Singapore Tourism Board; **15b** AA/N Setchfield; **16tr** Courtesy of Singapore Tourism Board; **16cr** AA/N Setchfield; **16bcr** AA/N Setchfield; **16br** AA/K Paterson; **17tl** AA/N Setchfield; **17cl** AA/A Kouprianoff; **17bcl** AA/N Setchfield; **17bl** AA/N Setchfield; **18tr** xPACIFICA/Alamy; **18cr** AA/N Setchfield; **18bcr** AA/N Setchfield; **18br** AA/N Setchfield; **19(i)** AA/N Setchfield; **19(ii)** Courtesy of Singapore Tourism Board; **19(iii)** AA/N Setchfield; **19(iv)** Courtesy of The Hantu Blog; **20/21** Sebastian Duda/Alamy; **24tl** AA/N Setchfield; **24tr** AA/N Setchfield; **24/25c** AA/N Setchfield; **25tr** AA/N Setchfield; **25cl** AA/N Setchfield; **25cr** AA/N Setchfield; **26l** Realimage/Alamy; **26r** Steve Hamblin/Alamy; **27l** AA/N Setchfield; **27r** AA/N Setchfield; **28tl** Alan Smithers/Alamy; **28bl** Jeff Greenberg/Alamy; **28/29** southeast asia/Alamy; **29t** Courtesy of Singapore Tourism Board; **29cr** AA/N Setchfield; **29cl** AA/N Setchfield; **30tl** AA/N Setchfield; **30tr** AA/N Setchfield; **31tl** AA/N Setchfield; **31tc** Courtesy of Singapore Tourism Board; **31tr** AA/N Setchfield; **32l** AA/N Setchfield; **32/33t** AA/N Setchfield; **32/33b** AA/N Setchfield; **33tr** Courtesy of Singapore Tourism Board; **33bl** AA/N Setchfield; **33br** AA/N Setchfield; **34** Horizon Images/Motion/Alamy; **35l** Courtesy of National Museum of Singapore; **35r** Courtesy of National Museum of Singapore; **36l** AA/N Setchfield; **36tr** AA/N Setchfield; **36br** Horizon Images/Motion/Alamy; **37t** Singapore Tourism Board; **37br** AA/N Setchfield; **38tl** AA/N Setchfield; **38tc** Courtesy of Media Bank; **38tr** AA/N Setchfield; **39tl** AA/N Setchfield; **39tc** AA/N Setchfield; **39tr** AA/N Setchfield; **40l** Courtesy of Singapore Flyer Pte Ltd; **40r** Courtesy of Singapore Flyer Pte Ltd; **41–44** AA/N Setchfield; **41l** AA/N Setchfield; **41r** AA/N Setchfield; **42l** Courtesy of Mint Museum of Toys; **42r** AA/N Setchfield; **43** Courtesy of Peranakan Museum; **44l** Courtesy of red dot Design Museum; **44r** AA/N Setchfield; **45** AA/N Setchfield; **46** AA/N Setchfield; **47** AA/N Setchfield; **48/49** Courtesy of Singapore Tourism Board; **50** AA/N Setchfield; **51** AA/N Setchfield; **52** AA/N Setchfield; **53** Courtesy of Singapore Tourism Board; **56tl** AA/N Setchfield; **56/57t** AA/N Setchfield; **56/57c** AA/N Setchfield; **56t** AA/N Setchfield; **57cl** AA/N Setchfield; **57cr** AA/N Setchfield; **58l** AA/N Setchfield; **58/59t** Courtesy of Singapore Tourism Board; **58/59b** SINGAPORE COLLECTION/Balan Madhavan/Alamy; **59t** Courtesy of Singapore Tourism Board; **59bl** AA/N Setchfield; **59br** AA/N Setchfield; **60** Courtesy of Singapore Zoo & Night Safari; **61t** Courtesy of Singapore Zoo & Night Safari; **61cl** Courtesy of Singapore Zoo & Night Safari; **61cr** Courtesy of Singapore Zoo & Night Safari; **62tl** AA/N Setchfield; **62bl** epa european pressphoto agency b.v./Alamy; **62/63** AA/A Kouprianoff; **63tr** AA/N Setchfield; **63br** age fotostock/Alamy; **64tl** AA/N Setchfield; **64tc** Courtesy of Singapore Discovery Centre; **64tr** AA/N Setchfield; **65** AA/N Setchfield; **66tl** AA/N Setchfield; **66/67c** AA/N Setchfield; **68tl** AA/N Setchfield; **68/69t** AA/N Setchfield; **68/69c** AA/N Setchfield; **69t** AA/N Setchfield; **69cl** AA/N Setchfield; **69cr** AA/N Setchfield; **70tl** Courtesy of Singapore Zoo & Night Safari; **70/71t** Courtesy of Singapore Zoo & Night Safari; **70/71c** Courtesy of Singapore Tourism Board; **71tl** Courtesy of Singapore Tourism Board; **71tr** Courtesy of Singapore Zoo & Night Safari; **71b** epa european pressphoto agency b.v./Alamy; **72–75t** AA/N Setchfield; **72bl** AA/N Setchfield; **72br** AA/N Setchfield; **73b** AA/N Setchfield; **74** AA/N Setchfield; **75l** AA/N Setchfield; **75r** AA/N Setchfield; **76** AA/N Setchfield; **77** AA/N Setchfield; **78** Courtesy of Singapore Tourism Board; **79** AA/N Setchfield; **82tl** Courtesy of Singapore Tourism Board; **82tr** AA/N Setchfield; **83tl** AA/N Setchfield; **83tr** AA/N Setchfield; **84tl** AA/N Setchfield; **84/85t** AA/N Setchfield; **84/85c** AA/N Setchfield; **85t** AA/N Setchfield; **85c** AA/N Setchfield; **86/87t** AA/N Setchfield; **86** AA/N Setchfield; **87bl** AA/N Setchfield; **87**br AA/N Setchfield; **88t** AA/N Setchfield; **89** AA/N Setchfield; **90t** AA/N Setchfield; **91t** Courtesy of Singapore Tourism Board; **92t** Courtesy of Singapore Tourism Board; **93** Courtesy of The Hantu Blog; **96tl** AA/N Setchfield; **96/97** AA/N Setchfield; **96bl** Courtesy of Singapore Tourism Board; **97** AA/N Setchfield; **98t** AA/N Setchfield; **98b** AA/N Setchfield; **99** AA/K Paterson; **100/101t** Courtesy of The Hantu Blog; **100bl** Courtesy of The Hantu Blog; **100cr** Courtesy of The Hantu Blog; **100br** Courtesy of The Hantu Blog; **101bl** Courtesy of The Hantu Blog; **101br** Courtesy of The Hantu Blog; **102t** AA/R Strange; **102bl** Leonid Serebrennikov/Alamy; **102br** Leonid Serebrennikov/Alamy; **103t** AA/N Setchfield; **103bl** AA/N Hanna; **103bcl** AA/N Setchfield; **103bc** AA/N Hanna; **103bcr** AA/N Setchfield; **103br** AA/N Setchfield; **104t** Courtesy of Singapore Tourism Board; **105t** AA/N Setchfield; **105c** Courtesy of Singapore Tourism Board; **106** AA/N Setchfield; **107** AA/N Setchfield; **108–112t** AA/C Sawyer; **108tr** Courtesy of Media Bank; **108tcr** Courtesy of Media Bank; **108cr** AA/N Ray; **108br** AA/N Setchfield; **113** Courtesy of Singapore Tourism Board; **114–125t** Courtesy of Singapore Tourism Board; **123** AA/N Setchfield; **124bl** AA/N Setchfield; **124bc** AA/N Setchfield; **124br** AA/N Setchfield; **125bl** AA/N Setchfield; **125bc** AA/N Setchfield; **125br** AA/N Setchfield

Every effort has been made to trace the copyright holders, and we apologise in advance for any accidental errors. We would be happy to apply the corrections in the following edition of this publication.